A GEOGRAPHY OF MODERN
Japan

Donald MacDonald
Lecturer in Geography, Jordanhill College of Education, Glasgow

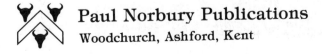

Paul Norbury Publications
Woodchurch, Ashford, Kent

Paul Norbury Publications Ltd
Woodchurch, Ashford, Kent TN26 3TW England

© Donald MacDonald 1985
First published 1985

ISBN 0-904404-43-9

Published with the kind assistance of
The Japan Foundation (Kokusai Koryu Kikin)

British Library C.I.P. Data
MacDonald, Donald, *1936–*
A geography of modern Japan.
1. Japan — Description and travel — 1945–
I. Title
915.2   DS811

ISBN 0-904404-43-9

General Adviser

John Sargent — Reader in Geography, School of Oriental &
African Studies, University of London

FRONT COVER: A major pedestrian interchange near Shibuya Station,
central Tokyo. (*Photo – Len Brown*)
BACK COVER: Senior high school students on a school visit to Kumamoto Castle,
Kumamoto Prefecture, Kyushu. (*Photo – Japan Library*)

Set in Century 11 on 12pt by Permanent Typesetting & Printing, Hong Kong.
Printed in England by A. Wheaton & Co. Ltd, Exeter, Devon

Contents

Foreword

For many years, those setting out to teach the geography of Japan, especially at the secondary-school level, have found their efforts frustrated by a lamentable shortage of textbooks and other published material suitable for use in the classroom. Of the few books available, many are out of date, and most are aimed mainly at university students. Moreover articles on Japan by professional geographers tend to be tucked away in specialist journals, and are hence out of reach to all but a few teachers.

This splendid book will therefore be widely welcomed. Donald Macdonald knows Japan well, and his writing is informed by first-hand field experience of the country. His treatment of the geography of Japan is concise yet admirably comprehensive: indeed several topics such as the service sector of the economy, social welfare issues, and living standards have never before been addressed properly in standard textbooks on the subject. Case studies are given wherever appropriate and reference is made to the applicability of western geographical models to Japanese circumstances. Perhaps the most attractive feature of the text is its happy blend of clarity and vividness. Donald Macdonald, more than most people, knows what is required of a successful textbook and he has the enviable knack of being able to summarize complicated issues in straightforward yet accurate terms.

Despite the increasing attention given to things Japanese in the mass media, and despite widespread awareness of Japanese economic achievements, Japan remains only patchily understood in most western countries. This book will do much to dispel many of the misconceptions which form part of the popular image of Japan and will introduce a wide audience to man-land relationships and their spatial consequences in a country that has been neglected for far too long by western geographers.

John Sargent

Fig. 1.1 *Faces of modern Japan*

1 The Population of Japan

Japan ranks among the world's largest countries by population, and its people form a distinctive group with a history unlike that of any other nation in Asia. The factors which have influenced the unique development of Japan's population can be analysed as follows.

Origins

It may seem easy to describe the appearance of a typical Japanese (Fig. 1.1). Rather smaller and more lightly-built than the average European, the Japanese usually have straight black hair, dark eyes with a noticeable skin fold, and skin of a light tan colour. Yet there are countless small differences, and to the Japanese themselves it is clear that the people of Japan do not have a common origin.

The islands of Japan were settled many thousands of years B.C. by Stone Age groups who were skilled hunters and gatherers. Remains of pottery, shells, stone arrowheads and fish hooks show that these early settlers lived mainly around the coasts. It seems likely that they came to Japan from at least three different sources.

One group probably came from the mainland of Siberia, to enter Japan from the north. Their descendants, the modern Ainu, differ in facial appearance from other Japanese, and it is only in recent years that the Ainu have become part of the main society. A second stream of early settlers seems to have come from China and Korea. Moving eastwards, these people brought with them a knowledge of wet rice growing and also of metal smelting. Again, from the islands of south-

east Asia and the Pacific, it is likely that a third great group of migrants reached southern Japan, over a long period of time. There has been little immigration into Japan over the past two thousand years, and from the various original sources a distinct ethnic group has now emerged – the modern Japanese.

Population factors

Except for the western nations of Europe, North America and Australasia, it is unusual to find a country which has been able to keep detailed records of population over many years. Japan is exceptional. Unlike every other nation in Asia, it has been conducting occasional nation-wide surveys of population since 1721. Ever since 1871, there has been quite an accurate system of registering households, whereby the annual numbers of births, deaths and marriages can be worked out. More recently, a full national census has been held every ten years (1920 to 1940) or every five years (from 1945 onwards). We can thus keep track (as in Fig. 1.2) of the way in which the Japanese population has been growing during the past two-and-a-half centuries. At the 1980 census, for example, the total population was close to 118 million, making Japan the seventh largest of the world's nations in terms of population. During the last twenty years, however, both Indonesia

Year	Population Total (millions)
1872	34.80 m.
1900	43.85 m.
1920	55.39 m.
1940	72.54 m.
1960	93.42 m.
1983	119.48 m.

Fig. 1.2 *Population growth in Japan, 1872-1983*

and Brazil have out-grown Japan.

Population growth is produced by two major factors: natural increase and net migration (the difference between the number of people entering the country and the number leaving it). For several centuries, Japan had no significant emigration or immigration, and it would thus be fair for us to concentrate mainly on natural increase. This is itself made up of the balance between annual birth rates and annual death rates.

Birth rates

All through the Middle Ages, it seems that Japan had a moderately high birth rate of about 25 per thousand people per year. Large families were common, because children were useful helpers on farms and could provide support in later years for aged parents. At the same time, the birth rate was kept down slightly by late marriages and by occasional famines, causing the loss of unborn babies. Then, from about 1870 on, more and more people began to move into industrial jobs in towns. Food shortages became rare, and a gradual rise in the birth rate appeared.

By 1920, the rate had reached a high level of 34.8, which is little short of the rates now found in the poorer developing countries. However, the difficult years of World War II brought about a temporary fall in the Japanese birth rate, which had declined to 23.0 by 1945. Then, as families were re-united after the war, the birth rate began to rise again. The sudden growth of population caused considerable concern to the Japanese government, which then passed the Eugenic Protection Law, allowing women to have legal abortions. A dramatic decline in the birth rate followed. By 1955, the rate (see Fig. 1.3) had fallen below 20.0, and over a million abortions per year were being carried out.

As the graph illustrates, the rate remained fairly steady thereafter, although there are three related features which

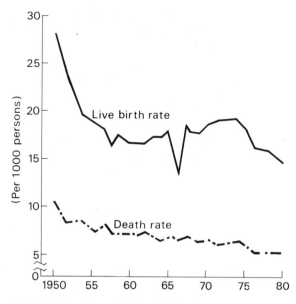

Fig. 1.3 *Japanese birth and death rates*

deserve attention. The first is a sudden sharp drop in 1966. According to the Japanese zodiac, that particular year was governed by Fire and Horse. Any female born under such a sign would be unlikely to have a happy life. Many Japanese couples obviously took this belief seriously, because 460,000 fewer babies were born in 1966 than in the previous

Fig. 1.4 *Family life in the 1980s*

year. There was then a slight temporary rise in the birth rate until 1974, and since then the trend has been clearly downwards.

The average family now has two children (Fig. 1.4). Compared with women in other advanced countries, Japanese women tend to marry later, when the peak of their fertility is past. Japan, then, is the only non-European country which, over a period of only thirty-five years, has gone through a quick transition from having a very high birth rate to having a low rate.

Death rates

For most of last century, when Japanese birth rates were high, death rates were also high. Indeed, a rate of between 21 and 19 per thousand occurred until the 1920s. A large proportion of the Japanese population lived in rural areas, where medical assistance was not easily available. In urban areas, too, public water supplies and sewage systems were poorly organised. Infectious diseases, such as tuberculosis and dysentery, were therefore common and the very young, as well as the old, were particularly at risk. Indeed, the infant mortality rate, which measures the number of deaths per year among children under one year of age, may at one time have been well over the 100 mark. By 1950, as Fig. 1.5 shows, the rate had come down towards 60, and from then on it has dropped to very low levels. The 1980

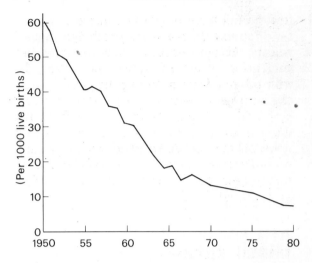

Fig. 1.5 *Infant mortality rate in Japan, 1950-80*

infant mortality rate of 8.7 is lower than that of Britain (Fig. 1.6) and it demonstrates that Japan is now an advanced nation with an excellent system of health care for young children.

The same improvements, of course, have affected the population as a whole. Good standards of feeding and modern medical facilities have helped to bring the national death rate steadily downwards, from its level of 11.0 in 1950 to 6.1 in 1980 (see Fig. 1.3). Few countries have death rates as low as this, and it would be fair to say that Japan is possibly the healthiest nation on earth at present. However, the low death rate is also caused by the fact that Japan is basically a youthful nation. As the population gradually ages and

Fig. 1.6 *International comparisons in infant mortality*

(per 1,000 persons)

	Japan	Canada	France	Germany (F.R.)	Italy	Singapore	United Kingdom	United States
1970	13.1	18.8	18.2	23.6	29.6	20.5	18.4	20.1
1971	12.4	17.6	17.1	23.3	28.5	20.1	17.9	19.1
1972	11.7	17.1	16.0	22.7	27.0	19.2	17.5	18.5
1973	11.3	15.6	15.5	22.9	25.7	20.3	17.2	17.7
1974	10.8	15.0	12.1	21.1	22.6	16.8	16.3	16.7
1975	10.1	15.0	12.6	19.8	20.7	13.9	16.0	16.1
1976	9.3	15.0	10.4	17.4	19.1	11.6	14.3	15.1
1980	7.5	10.9	10.0	12.6	14.3	11.7	12.1	12.5

Source: Monthly Bulletin of Statistics, U.N. and Statistical Yearbook, U.N.

fewer children are born, the death rate tends to rise slightly. The aging population will be vulnerable to the fatal illnesses, such as strokes, cancers and heart trouble, which have been prevalent for so long in the western world.

Natural increase

The natural increase per year in any country is easily worked out by subtracting the death rate from the birth rate. As a rule, the result is given as a percentage. Throughout the earlier decades of the twentieth century, the rate of natural increase in Japan varied between 1.0 and 1.6 per cent. During the period of World War II, the death rate rose while the birth rate fell, and for a brief spell there was no natural increase. Then, in the post-war years, natural increase very quickly became established again. Additional population pressure was caused by the return of about five million Japanese from former overseas colonies. But the rapid rate of increase did not last long. It slowed down as family planning took effect. More recently, the annual rate of natural increase has reached levels as low as 0.7 per cent, and may well fall still further.

The Graph of Demographic Transition

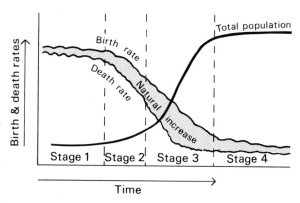

Fig. 1.7 *Demographic transition*

(Fig. 1.7) is widely used to show the changing pattern of natural increase in an advanced country. For Japan, the three stages of the graph do seem to apply, although two features set Japan somewhat apart. There was a sharper increase between Stages 1 and 2 than in the model. Furthermore, the decline in birth rates, and hence in natural increase, took place more quickly than the model would suggest.

Population structure

Every country has, at a given time, a distinct population structure. Pyramid

Fig. 1.8 *Japanese population pyramids, past, present and future*

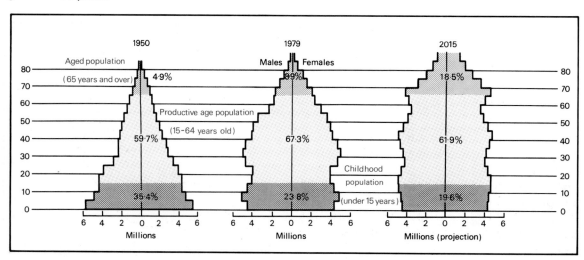

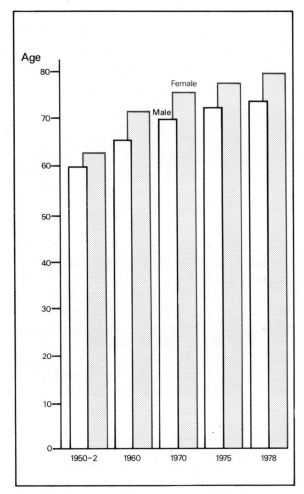

Fig. 1.9 *Japanese life expectancy, 1950-78*

Life expectancy

There is evidence, as seen in Fig. 1.9, that the average life expectancy of Japanese men and women is continuing to rise, helped by high all-round standards of health. Indeed, the graph (Fig. 1.10) suggests that the Japanese can expect to have a higher proportion of aged inhabitants than any other nation. However, the steady aging of the population brings with it two awkward problems. For one thing, there will be fewer young workers available in the future, although this may not turn out to be such a serious difficulty, since there may be fewer jobs to be filled. A more disturbing question is whether the ever-increasing need to provide care for the elderly can always be met. Not only will they require medical facilities, day leisure centres and old folks' homes, but many will also look for part-time jobs.

Density of population

Population density, measured in persons per square kilometre, shows the degree of crowding in any country. At first glance, Japan seems to be just one of a group of countries, all of which are very densely populated. But these figures (Fig. 1.11) are

Fig. 1.10 *Increasing proportions of aged people in selected countries (65 years and over)*

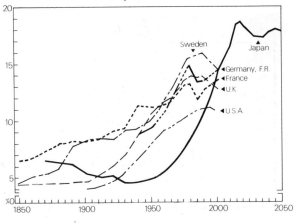

diagrams are the most common means of showing how a population is made up, with different numbers of males and females in different age groups. Looking at the three Japanese population pyramids in Fig. 1.8, you will see two noteworthy features. One is the fact that Japan in 1979 had over two-thirds of its population in the productive age-group-more than any other country in the world. Secondly, there is the change taking place in both the upper and lower sections of the pyramid. The proportion of younger people is clearly decreasing, while the proportion of older Japanese is certainly going to be much more obvious as time goes on.

Fig. 1.12 *Kobe city and surrounding mountains. Note the 'urban sprawl' taking place up the moutain-side.*

not quite as simple as they appear. The Netherlands, for example, has a fairly even spread of population, and few parts of that country are empty. Japan, on the other hand, presents a very different picture. Most of the land surface is made up of forested mountain and hill slopes, very lightly populated. There is therefore great pressure on the coastal plains and basins (see Fig. 1.12), where more than two-thirds of the population live.

Thus, the population density which many Japanese actually experience daily is far higher than the figure quoted above.

Indeed, the only other parts of the world with densities similar to Japan are the city-states of Singapore and Hong Kong which are far too small to be genuinely compared with a nation like Japan.

Fig. 1.13 *Population densities in regions of Japan, 1978*

Fig. 1.11 *International comparisons in population density, 1977*

Country	Density (persons per sq. km.)
South Korea	370
Netherlands	339
Belgium	325
Japan	306
West Germany	247
U.K.	229
India	187
Denmark	118

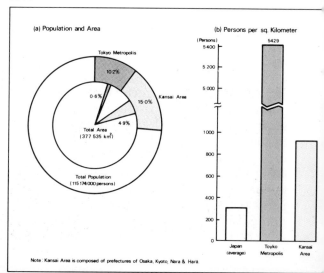

(a) Population and Area

Tokyo Metropolis

10·2%

0·6%

Kansai Area

15·0%

4·9%

Total Area
(377 535 km²)

Total Population
(115 174 000 persons)

(b) Persons per sq. Kilometer

(Persons)

5400

5429

5 200

5 000

1000

800

600

400

200

0

Japan
(average)

Toyko
Metropolis

Kansai
Area

Note : Kansai Area is composed of prefectures of Osaka, Kyoto, Nara & Hara.

High density makes itself felt in a number of ways. Officially, it has been recognised ever since the 1960 census, in which densely inhabited districts (DIDs) were first instituted. The three largest concentrations of DIDs are Metropolitan Tokyo (taking a 70-kilometre radius from the city centre); Osaka (a 50-kilometre radius from the centre) and Nagoya (also a 50-km radius). In these areas (see Fig. 1.13), population densities can reach 5000 per square kilometre, whereas the least crowded Japanese prefecture, Hokkaido, has a density of only 70. Less official, but nonetheless real, is the acute sense of overcrowding which European visitors feel in the thronged streets and railway stations of Japan's cities (Fig. 1.14).

Urbanisation

High population densities, as we have seen, are common in urban Japan. In the early Meiji period, from 1868 onwards, the towns and cities of Japan contained only a small fraction of the total population. At

Fig. 1.14 *A festival day in crowded Japan*

Fig. 1.15 *Osaka castle (castle town)*

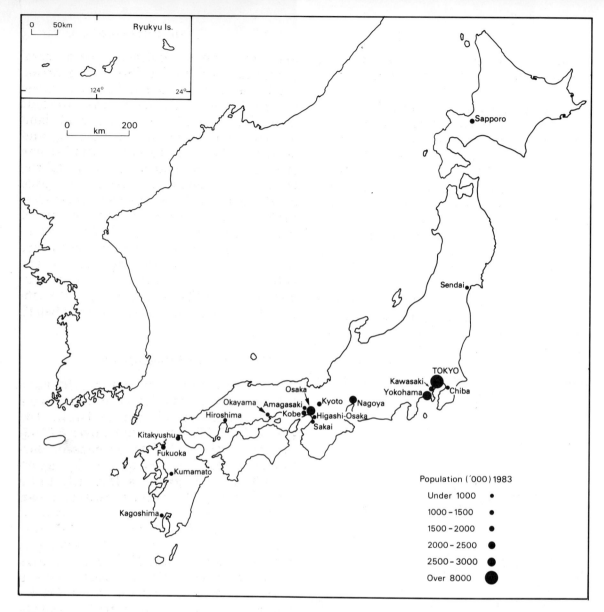

City	Population (000s)		
Tokyo (ward area)	8151	Kyoto	1461
Yokohama	2868	Kobe	1370
Osaka	2535	Sapporo	1451
Nagoya	2058	Kitakyushu	1055
		Fukuoka	1082
		Kawasaki	1039

Fig. 1.16 *Major cities of Japan*

that time, over 90 per cent of all Japanese used to live in the countryside, on dispersed farms or more commonly in village clusters. Yet, urban settlements had been established from an early date. Planned cities, such as the two ancient capitals of Nara and Kyoto, were founded in the eighth century. Temple towns (*monzen-machi*), which also acted as market centres, were found widely, as were castle towns (*joka-machi*) (Fig. 1.15). Again, along the main land routes of the nation, stage towns (*shukuba-machi*) grew up. Thus, the great Tokaido road between Tokyo and Kyoto had 53 such settlements. Furthermore, during the eighteenth century, three of the main Japanese cities were among the biggest urban places in the world. Tokyo (or Edo, as it was then called) may have had up to one million inhabitants, while Kyoto and Osaka were probably half that size.

It was after 1870, when Japan was opening up to world trade once again, that modern industrial settlements began to develop. By 1900, Japan had 166 towns and cities with a populations of 10,000 or more, and by 1920 there were no fewer than 232 towns and cities, containing over a third of the entire population. Not every developing city· was an industrial centre, like Kawasaki, Hitachi or Yawata. Some were commercial ports, such as Kobe and Yokohama, or naval centres, like Kure and Sasebo.

The growth of the urban population in Japan has continued right through the present century and has been accompanied by some notable features. None of these is by any means peculiar to Japan alone, but no other country shows all the features as clearly as does Japan.

1. *The rural-urban exodus*

In the early years of modern urban growth, most of the new city dwellers came originally from the countryside. Thus, between 1870 and 1970, the population of Japan was completely redistributed. In 1870, only about eight per cent lived in towns and cities having more than 10,000 inhabitants. A century later, by contrast, 52 per cent were living in metropolitan centres having over 100,000 inhabitants. Meanwhile, rural districts have lost the huge share of the population which they once had. Between 1950 and 1975, for example, several of the remote prefectures in Kyushu, Shikoku, Hokuriku (Western Honshu) and Tohoku (Northern Honshu) were showing clear decreases in population. On a national scale, while there were 48.6 million rural dwellers in 1955, the total had fallen to 32 million by 1975.

2. *Suburban sprawl*

The cities of Japan have been growing rapidly, not only in population size but also in extent. Indeed, where rural migrants once flooded into urban areas, the tendency nowadays is for urban areas to sprawl outwards across the adjacent farmlands (Fig. 1.12). Valuable arable land is continually being lost to housing, and outlying villages and small towns become stitched into the spreading urban fabric. Overall, the demand for usable land space is more acute in Japan than anywhere else. Linked to this, in turn, is the problem of long-distance commuting. To find accommodation at a reasonable price, people are forced to buy houses far out on the suburban fringe. Journeys to work can last over two hours each way, and rush-hour trains are overcrowded beyond belief.

3. *The growth of megalopolis*

The major Japanese cities (Fig. 1.16) have taken in a truly vast influx of inhabitants since the end of World War II. During the period 1955–75, for example, over 37 million new citizens had to be housed. Surprisingly, perhaps, no single city apart from Tokyo has grown sufficiently to be ranked among the world's greatest urban centres. At the same time, there has been a distinct tendency for cities to ˝grow gradually into one another. For example, Tokyo, Yokohama and Kawasaki are part of one vast conurbation. Similarly, there is virtually no break between Kobe, Osaka and Kyoto, These in turn reach towards Nagoya, and the entire east coast urban area which has emerged is sometimes known as the Tokaido megalopolis.

4. *Urban difficulties*

Since the larger urban centres have been populated by people from all over Japan, it seems that city dwellers until recently have often shown little concern about local issues. In particular, this lack of concern has meant that Japanese cities are not usually well planned. Houses, for example, are packed into crowded, untidy groupings and there are frequently no street names

Fig. 1.17 *Typical mixture of urban land uses in Japan — a conglomeration of roads, railways, elevated expressways mixed with houses, factories small workshops and flats*

or house numbers. Similarly, the older areas of Japanese towns in many cases resemble old-fashioned villages, because they have no proper sewage systems or paved footpaths. Again, housing areas are mixed (see Fig. 1.17) with railway lines, factories and workshops in such a way that noise and pollution have become serious problems for many city folk.

Migration

High densities of population have been common in Japan. Yet there has never been any easy solution to this problem. Unlike many other nations, the Japanese have not been much affected by emigra-

tion (or, for that matter, by immigration). However, there have been two noticeable streams of migration from Japan to overseas destinations. One group of migrants began to leave soon after Japan (closed to outside contact since the early seventeenth century) was re-opened in the late 1860s.

Landless rural labourers were offered work in the new sugar and pineapple plantations of Hawaii, while others went on to the farmlands of California. Their descendants today make up a recognisable minority in the Pacific states of the U.S.A., numbering 0.3 million. Meanwhile, a second group of Japanese found their way to Brazil, which now has over half a million people of Japanese ancestry among its population. Most of these have settled in southern Brazil, between Sao

Paulo and Rio Grande do Sul. Others have become spice growers along the Amazon River, in Para state. Here, settlement had begun in the 1930s, and increased considerably after World War II. Japanese who had been repatriated to their homeland from parts of the former empire, such as Manchuria, Malaysia and Indo-China, began to look for new opportunities. At that time, Brazil was one of the very few countries willing to accept Japanese settlers.

But in the years since 1945, emigration has not been a real alternative for most Japanese. Although thousands do work in the overseas offices of Japanese firms, almost all return home after serving two or three years. One has to add that the thought of leaving their native land for ever is generally abhorred by the Japanese. So, no matter how crowded Japan has become, its people have had little choice but to make the best of it. One traditional way of doing this has been seasonal migration. Thus, part-time farmers from the north and west regularly use the winter season to take temporary jobs in sawmills, breweries or on assembly lines elsewhere in Japan. Again, as we have seen, millions of people have chosen to migrate from the more backward regions of Japan to urban areas of greater prosperity.

2 The Natural Environment

Landscapes

Japan lies off the eastern coast of Asia. Its four main islands of Hokkaido, Honshu, Shikoku and Kyushu offer a wide range of beautiful scenery. Most of the country is upland, and much of the upland is made up of volcanoes, both old and new. To understand the main features of Japan's landscapes, we can take a detailed look at five different types of scenery. Fig. 2.1 lets you see where these areas are located within Japan.

1. The Hida Range

On a clear winter day in Central Honshu,

Fig. 2.1 *Japan: location of five selected landscapes and main tectonic lines*

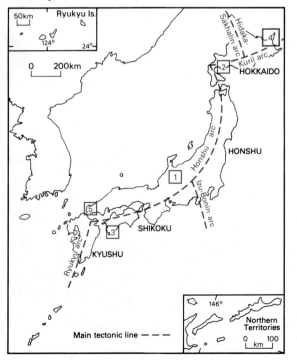

the view (see Fig. 2.2) across the windswept mountain peaks of the Hida Range is most dramatic. As far as the eye can see, high ridges interlock with each other in such a way that the word 'chain' seems to be very applicable. The underlying rocks, where they appear, are dark grey with a purplish tinge. In the main, however, they are hidden. The higher slopes, above 2000 metres, are partly covered by irregular blankets of snow and ice. Lower down, most of the surface is concealed by a spread of coniferous forest. Above everything else stands the sharp peak of Mount Tsurugi-dake. Jagged ridges radiate out and downwards from it to the valleys far below. Above the Higashizawa Valley, a huge ice-filled bowl reflects the January sunshine. Its local name is Noguchi-goro. Gazing across this scene, the western visitor is reminded of similar mountain landscapes in the Alps.

When we come to explain the Hida landscape, we must first remember that Japan lies at a specially active node on the earth's crust, as Fig. 2.3 shows. Here, no fewer than three of the world's giant tectonic plates (Eurasian, Pacific and Philippine) adjoin. As these vast plates slowly move, over millions of years, they produce forces powerful enough to build mountain chains close to the plate boundaries. The result is that the backbone of Honshu has been forced upwards in the Akaishi, Kiso and Hida ranges which form the Japan Alps.

In the same way, upraised mountain systems can be traced right through Japan, from Kyushu all the way north to Hokkaido. However, mountain building alone does not explain the jagged outline of the Alpine peaks of Central Honshu. A second important factor in shaping the

Fig. 2.2 *Glaciated valley of the Higashizawa River, Japan Alps*

Fig. 2.3 *Volcanic activity and mountain building at the junction of tectonic plates*

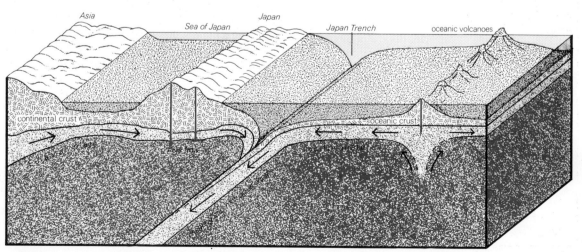

landscape has been the weathering that results from heavy rainfall, especially during the summer months, as well as from wide annual and daily changes in temperature. By contrast with Europe and North America, the impact of the Ice Age upon the mountain landscape has been slight.

2. Lake Toya

In the south-western corner of the island of Hokkaido lies a circular lake, about ten kilometres across (Fig. 2.4). Round the edge of the lake runs a rim of hilly land, about two hundred metres high. Towards the southern side, the scene changes. Here, Mount Usu looms above the lake. Steam seeps hissing from its upper slopes, and the air all around carries the stench of sulphur. A short distance away from Mount Usu stands the bare lumpy crag of Showa Shinzan, tinted with a mixture of dark red, brown and grey. Jets of vapour keep shifting across its multi-coloured bulk. An occasional molten gleam shows through the rocks and suggests that this landscape is in some kind of torment. Out in the centre of Lake Toya, on the other hand, the scene is more placid. A round island sits precisely in the centre of the lake. Two steep hills, tree-clad to their tops, occupy most of the island and on calm days their shapes are reflected clearly in the still water.

Volcanic action is the key to the Lake Toya landscape. Japan's position on the unstable margin of the Pacific allows molten material from the earth's interior

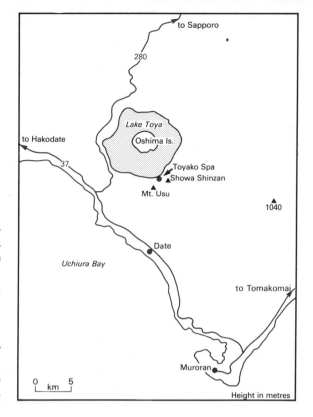

Fig. 2.5 *Lake Toya and its surroundings*

to seep outwards in a number of places. Devastating eruptions are rare, but during the past million or so years there have been several massive volcanic explosions. On occasion, entire mountain tops have been blown into dusty fragments, leaving behind circular craters like the one now occupied by Lake Toya. Such craters often fill up with water, to form the sort of lake which is common in Hokkaido. Continuing volcanic activity can then create newer peaks, which protrude as islands above the surface of the lake.

Fig. 2.4 *Lake Toya*

Fig. 2.6 *Southern Shikoku: general location*

and thousands of people had to be evacuated from their homes.

3. Tatsukushi

The coast of Tatsukushi lies in south-western Shikoku (see Fig. 2.6). Offshore, small islets dot the Bungo Channel, which stretches across to the distant shores of Kyushu. Looking along the Shikoku coastline (Fig. 2.7), you immediately notice that it is made up of huge natural steps or terraces. The topmost level is well over 100 metres above the sea, while far below stand lesser steps, at about ten and twenty metres. Walking along at this lower level, you see that the local rock is a light-brown shade and that it breaks easily into fragments. Inland, where the uppermost terrace disappears into the hilly interior of the island, a thick cover of low evergreen forest hides much of the surface. Away to the east, Cape Ashizuri is almost lost in a salt-tasting haze, where Shikoku meets the emerald-green waters of the Pacific.

Around Lake Toya (see Fig. 2.5), there are many signs that volcanic action is still going on. Mount Usu, for example, is constantly on the boil and occasionally shows flashes of real fury. Violent eruptions in August 1977 covered the surrounding countryside with hot dust

Fig. 2.7 *Shikoku coastline*

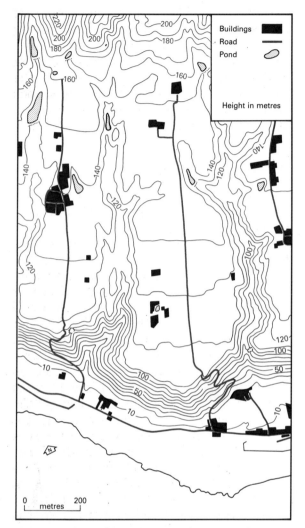

Fig. 2.8 *The Nishiyama area: a typical coastal district of southern Shikoku*

This terraced coastline of Shikoku has been produced by changes in the level of the sea. As the last Ice Age came to an end, immense quantities of water were released, helping to raise the sea level around Japan. Beaches were created at this high level. Then the sea began to fall again, as mountain-building forces gradually uplifted the Japanese islands. As a result, the former beach-lines now stand high and dry (Fig. 2.8). On Shikoku, the lower terraces are intensively cultivated. However, the slopes leading up to the highest terrace are too steep to be farmed and have therefore remained under forest.

We have already seen areas of Japan which were composed either of volcanic materials or of ancient rocks. But there are other parts of the country where the underlying rocks are sedimentary layers of quite recent origin. One such area is southern Shikoku, where sandstones and clays are common. Overall, Japan has few extensive lowlands; those which do exist are therefore very important for human settlement. Among these are the Kanto Plain, surrounding Tokyo, the Nobi Plain around Nagoya and the Ishikari lowlands of western Hokkaido. See Fig. 2.9.

4. Shiretoko Peninsula

The peninsula of Shiretoko (Fig. 2.10) juts out for 60 kilometres into the Sea of Okhotsk, like a giant stone thumb. Along the spine of the peninsula runs a high irregular ridge, with occasional mountain peaks reaching over 1500 metres. The views from these mountain tops are among the most dramatic in all Japan. To the north, the coastline sweeps away in a smooth curve as far as one can see. To the

Fig. 2.9 *Japan: major lowland areas*

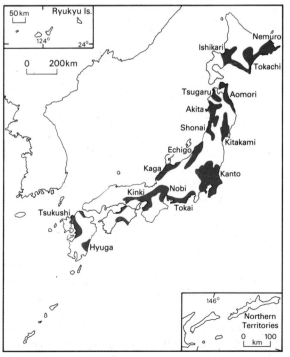

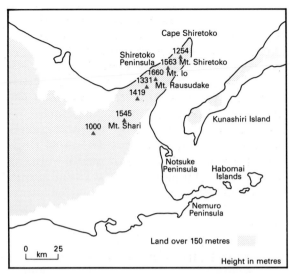

Fig. 2.10 *Location of the Shiretoko Peninsula*

currents to make a low-lying curve of beach and marsh. The fourth process affecting Shiretoko is change in sea level, which has left former beaches standing well above the present shoreline of the peninsula. Thus it is that the landscapes of this area have been formed by a combination of physical processes.

5. Akiyoshi-dai

The south-western extremity of the main island of Honshu is usually referred to as Chugoku. The coastline here is quite densely populated, but the interior uplands are sparsely settled. In particular, the plateau of Akiyoshi-dai is unusually desolate. Anyone who has walked across the fells and dales of the Pennines would feel more or less at home here. The air may be warm and clammy, but these high Japanese tablelands have the same springy turf as the Peak District in England. Everywhere there is a litter of grey-white stone slabs, so that you get the impression of being in some gigantic disorderly graveyard. No rivers run across this surface, but there are many sink-holes which lead underground through endless tunnels and caverns. Akiyoshi-dai is within 30 kilometres of towns, railways, holiday resorts and rich croplands, so it is all the more surprising that its landscape should lie almost untouched.

Any explanation of the Akiyoshi landscape must mention the nature of the underlying rocks. Far back in the geological past, thick layers of limestone were laid down in the shallow seas which covered parts of present-day Japan. Limestone is thus widely found, from Okinawa in the far south to Gifu in the centre and Aomori in the north. Water passes easily through limestone, causing the interior of the rock to partly dissolve. The surface remains dry. This in turn means that only a thin cover of soil will form and grasses will be the dominant type of plant. The land is of very little use for agriculture. Great earth movements have pushed the limestone layers upwards to form the

south, about 20 kilometres offshore, lies an island which is roughly the same size and shape as the peninsula itself. On this side, too, the main trend of the Hokkaido coast runs in a gentle arc, away from Shiretoko. Out on the cape, at the farthest end of this bleak peninsula, dark stepped cliffs overlook an angry sea. Winter comes early here, to bring drifting ice which locks this remote coast in frozen silence.

To explain the Shiretoko landscape, we have to refer to four different processes. The first is mountain-building, which has created an upland spine running through south-eastern Hokkaido, Shiretoko and on into Kunashiri and the other islands of the Kuriles chain. The second process, closely related to the first, is volcanic action which has produced the individual mountain peaks on the peninsula. Third, there are the ocean currents which have created the coastlines on either side of Shiretoko. To the north, cold coastal currents sweep down from Sakhalin, bringing winter ice floes.

Over many thousands of years, waves have smoothed out the coastline. Former inlets of the sea are now blocked off by sandbars, creating salty lagoons. Similarly, on the south side of Shiretoko, mud and sand are carried along by coastal

Fig. 2.11 *The river as a landscape element (Tone river, Gumma Prefecture)*

Coastal erosion and deposition

We have already noted that some coastal areas of Japan have emerged from the sea since the last Ice Age. Meanwhile, other areas have been submerged, to form the many rias or drowned valleys of the Pacific coast. Again, the sea has clearly been destroying some coasts, as at Cape Tappi in northern Honshu, while building up others, such as the Tottori sand dunes in the south. Adding to all this variety is the fact that Japan extends over such a wide band of latitude. This in turn means that coasts vary from the icy headlands of northern Hokkaido to the sub-tropical coral reefs of the Ryukyu Islands, which trail like a necklace from the south of the country.

River erosion and deposition

Since Japan is a mountainous country, with a generally heavy annual rainfall, there are numerous rivers (Fig. 2.11) running from the interior uplands to the sea. These rivers have sculpted the mountains, producing narrow 'V'-shaped valleys which then link up with wider valleys, where the rivers deposit their silt and mud. Alluvial features are common throughout Japan, although no single Japanese river is of any great size. Waterfalls and rapids are part of the upland scene. By contrast, river flood-plains and deltas make up much of the most useful land around the coasts.

rugged plateau of Akiyoshi-dai. These same movements were active elsewhere in Japan, producing uplands and exposing enormous masses of granite in several localities. However, this entire period is commonly referred to as the Akiyoshi uplift.

Other factors in the natural landscape

In the five areas we have been considering, we were able to identify certain forces at work in the landscapes of Japan. Among these forces are mountain-building, volcanic action, glaciation and sea-level changes. Each of these has helped to shape the scenery of modern Japan. However, we have to remember that other factors have also played an important part.

The work of rivers and the sea, then, has made a clear contribution to the richly varied landscapes of Japan. But the basic foundation has been laid by volcanic action and by mountain-building, both caused by movements in the earth's crust. No other nation has so many active volcanoes 'about 80' in such a relatively small area, and cone-shaped mountains such as Mount Fuji are in fact often seen as symbols of the Japanese landscape.

Climate

The Japanese climate is unlike that of any other area, except perhaps the east coast of the United States. To see why this should be the case, we need to understand the main factors which affect Japan's climate.

1. General location

The most obvious feature of Japan's position is that it lies between 24°N and 42°N.* Its extent is thus roughly the same as that between the Canary Islands and the south of France (Fig. 2.12). On this basis alone, you might expect Japan to have a distinctly sub-tropical climate in the south, and a Mediterranean climate in the north. The reality, however, is quite different, because it is affected by a number of other factors.

2. Nearness to Siberia

The Japanese islands lie not far to the east of Siberia, and the severe winter conditions which occur in the Siberian interior

Fig. 2.12 *Japan on the same scale as North Africa and Western Europe*

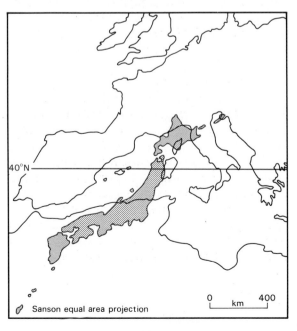

Sanson equal area projection

0 km 400

* Japanese maps, on the other hand, show a position of 45°N because within its borders Japan includes what it calls the Northern Territories which consist of four main islands off the north-east coast of Hokkaido — Habomais, Shikotan, Kunashiri and Etorofu. These islands have been occupied by the USSR since the end of World War II. We have shown these islands in a box on maps throughout this book.

exert a marked effect on winter weather throughout Japan. Northern Honshu, for example, has winter days when the maximum temperature does not even climb to freezing point, while the far north of Hokkaido has, on average, 70 such days per annum.

3. Ocean surroundings

The Japanese climate is also affected by the seas which surround the country. Hence, the atmosphere is usually moist, and the relative humidity averages 75% in winter, rising to 85% in summer. One result is that Japan, even at the very height of summer, is a land of greenery. The seas around the country have another effect, in that they delay the rise of temperatures in spring and summer, so that the hottest month is August. Yet again, ocean currents play a part, which is important enough to consider separately.

4. Ocean currents

The islands of Japan, as shown in the map (Fig. 2.13), lie amidst a giant whirl of branching and inter-mingling ocean currents. Two of these are especially powerful. The warm Kuroshio, or 'black current', flows northwards from the central Pacific, while its chilly counter-part, the Oyashio, or 'parent current', runs south from the Bering Sea. These currents and their various branches have the following effects on the climate of Japan.

(i) The Kuroshio and its offshoot, the Tsushima current, help to raise the temperatures of places along the western and south-eastern coasts of Japan.

(ii) The Oyashio lowers the tem-

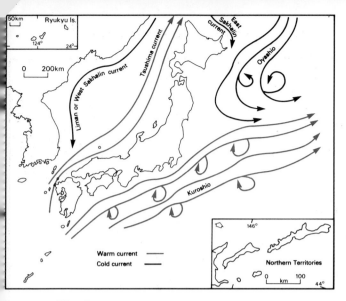

Fig. 2.13 *Ocean currents affecting Japan*

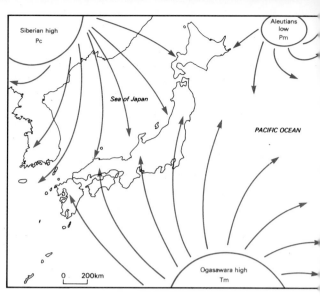

Fig. 2.14 *Air masses affecting Japan*

peratures of places around the coasts of Hokkaido and north-eastern Honshu.

(iii) The Tsushima current and the Kuroshio act as guidelines for tropical storms, and typhoon tracks often follow the warm currents very closely.

(iv) The warm water of the Tsushima current provides heating and uplift to the polar continental air from Siberia which crosses the Japan Sea in winter. Cloud then forms and precipitation is increased along the west coast of Japan.

(v) Numerous effects are produced locally by ocean currents. One example is the Soya Straits fog, which is almost as serious a menace as that of the New-foundland Grand Banks. It forms where warm air from the surface of the Tsushima current is suddenly cooled on meeting the frigid flow of the East Sakhalin current.

5. Contrasting air masses

Another important feature of the Japanese climate is that the country is affected by large masses of air (Fig. 2.14), which originate in regions far removed from Japan. These air masses then bring the distinctive characteristics of their source regions with them, during their movement towards Japan. In particular, three air masses occur quite frequently.

(i) *Polar continental*

This air mass forms in the wastes of Central Siberia. It is strongly developed in winter, but weak in summer. From it blow steady north-west winds, which are dry and bitterly cold. Crossing the Sea of Japan in winter, this polar continental air picks up moisture. On reaching the hilly west coast, the damp and unstable air forms heavy cloud and produces frequent snow showers. However, on passing over the mountain ranges of Honshu, the air becomes drier again, and so on the Pacific side the winter weather is usually fine and clear, though there are severe radiation frosts by night.

(ii) *Tropical maritime*

Like the polar continental air of winter, this summer air mass develops in a high pressure system or anti-cyclone. In this case, the pressure system, known as the Ogasawara high, is centred over the North Pacific. From it blow southerly and south-westerly winds which carry very warm moist air across the islands of Japan, covering the whole country by the end of July or early August. In winter, the Ogasawara high pressure system becomes weaker and its air then affects only the extreme south of the country, as a rule.

Over the course of the year, tropical

maritime air produces two rather different types of weather in Japan. When it first moves northwards across the country in late spring, tropical maritime air meets cooler polar maritime air, and a zone of cloud and rain forms where the two air masses meet. The wet spell which follows is often known as *Bai-u* (=plum-rain) or 'the season of mould', in Japan. However, this frontal zone (Fig. 2.15) gradually moves away northwards as the summer progresses, and from then on the tropical maritime air creates very warm conditions, with prolonged sunshine and haze throughout most of the country.

(iii) *Polar maritime*

The Sea of Okhotsk, to the far north of Japan, is a source region for a third type of air mass, known as polar maritime. This air is whirled outwards in the low pressure systems which cross Japan from time to time, especially during the late winter, spring and early summer. Polar maritime

Fig. 2.15 *A typical weather situation during the Bai-u rainy season*

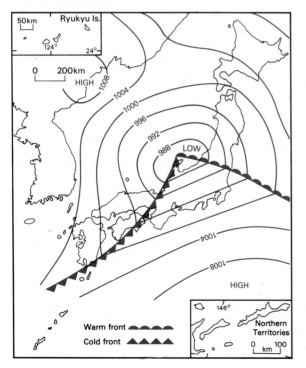

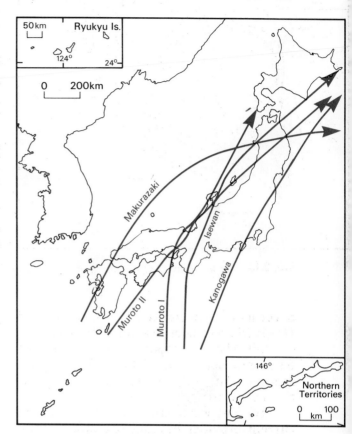

Fig. 2.16 *Tracks of selected typhoons*

air is usually cool and moist. It brings to Japan a mixture of showery weather and dry, clear spells. Of the three main air masses affecting Japan during the year, polar maritime would tend to be the least common.

Climatic variation

The Japanese climate, then, is produced by a number of factors working together. However, the climate is itself subject to two kinds of variation. The first is seasonal change, which is quite clearly defined in Japan and is often thought of as one of life's pleasures. Spring is seen as marking the start of the climatic year in Japan. It begins with the gradual weakening of the polar continental air mass and the first appearance of tropical maritime air. This air mass is then dominant throughout the summer, weakens during the autumn and

Fig. 2.17 *Flooding in Kumamoto Prefecture*

is replaced in winter by polar continental air. Changes in clothing and food go along with the changes in seasonal climate. The other important variation is found between one part of the country and another.

Weather and climate hazards

Japan happens to be one of the most naturally dangerous countries in the world. This does not mean to say that the Japanese go about in constant fear of their

lives. Far from it. But there are several natural hazards which do affect the country and its inhabitants from time to time. Some of these problems are connected with weather, and act over a short period of time, while others have to do with climate and take effect over a number of weeks or even months.

1. *Tropical storms*

Typhoons are large whirling storms which

Fig. 2.18 *Typhoons of modern times*

Date	Locality	Dead and Lost	Houses destroyed
Sept. 17, 1945	W. Japan	2,405	113,438
Sept. 14, 1947	Kanto, Tohoku	1,910	5,301
Sept. 15, 1948	Kanto, Tohoku	2,308	16,683
Oct. 13, 1951	Setouchi	3,587	70,512
Sept. 26, 1954	N. Japan	3,362	29,776
Sept. 26, 1958	Kanto	1,324	1,084
Sept. 26, 1959	Central Japan	5,207	35,125
Sept. 13-18, 1965	Countrywide	181	1,879
Sept. 23-25, 1966	Countrywide (*Except Hokkaido*)	317	2,422
Aug. 15-18, 1968	Kinki & Chubu	119	64
July 3-11, 1974	Countrywide (*Except Tohoku & Hokkaido*)	146	657
Sept. 8-17, 1976	Countrywide (*Especially Kagawa & Okayama*)	171	1,669
Oct. 14-22, 1979	Countrywide	115	139
July 31-Aug. 2, 1982	Kyushu, Kinki & Chubu	439	1,120
Sept. 10-12, 1982	Tokai, Kanto, Chubu & Hokkaido	35	130

form in the warm moist atmosphere over the North Pacific, between the Equator and the Tropic of Cancer. The typhoon season begins as the ocean is warming up to its maximum temperature in August. Thus, between June and October, typhoons are liable to come raging in towards the Asian continent. As the map (Fig. 2.16) shows, Japan lies in the general track of these Pacific storms. As a typhoon approaches, its fierce winds sweep thick cloud and torrential rain over the densely-populated lowlands of Japan. High waves smash across the shoreline, damaging small craft. The salt water can also destroy crops growing on coastal farmland. Rice is beginning to ripen at this time of the year, and is therefore vulnerable to damage. Further inland, the exceptionally heavy rainfall causes flooding (Fig. 2.17), and here, too, crops and homes are at risk.

To offset the danger, every one of Japan's forty-seven prefectures has its own plans for the prevention of disastrous flooding during the typhoon season. Meanwhile, warnings of approaching typhoons are given by the Japan Meteorological Agency. In recent years, however, the loss of life caused by typhoons has not been as severe as in the years following World War II (see Fig. 2.18).

2. *Winter depressions*

Japan is also susceptible to damage from mid-latitude depressions, which are less intense than their tropical counterparts, the Pacific typhoons. These depressions are a particular problem in winter along the Japan Sea coast (Fig. 2.19), and are more severe in the north than in the south. Driving rain accompanies howling gales of up to 100 kilometres per hour. Where these are channelled by the shape of the land, they can cause considerable damage to sea-walls, houses and coastal forests.

Fig. 2.19 *The result of flooding and high winds*

Climatic station	Precipitation (mm per year)	Evapo-transpiration (mm per year)
Naha	2222	1648
Hiroshima	1596	1222
Kanazawa	2560	1040
Nagano	1001	1130
Tokyo	1563	1063
Sendai	1232	940

Fig. 2.20 *The balance between precipitation and evapo-transpiration in Japan*

The ferry service across the Tsugaru Straits, for example, is liable to disruption at these times, and fishing operations also come to a temporary halt.

3. Floods

Typhoons, as we have seen, produce flooding by tidal surges along the coast and by heavy rainfall further inland. However, typhoons are not the only cause of floods, which are the most common type of weather hazard in Japan. Other causes include:

(i) The *Bai-u* rains can be exceptionally heavy in certain years.

(ii) During some summers there may be very frequent thunderstorms, with occasional downpours so heavy that one could imagine some enormous basin in the heavens being tipped over.

(iii) The melting of winter snows may begin quite suddenly, during an abrupt rise of temperature in early March. Hence, upland streams can soon turn into brimming torrents. Since many such streams drain on to densely inhabited lowlands, the likelihood of flood damage is perhaps greater in Japan than anywhere else in the world.

Whatever their cause, floods in their turn cause various other natural disasters, such as mudflows and landslides.

4. Snowfall

Blizzards and drifting snow are a possibility during winter months, especially along the west coast of Japan and on the island of Hokkaido. It would not be entirely fair to describe these events as weather hazards, since a hazard is an unexpected happening. Japan is usually prepared for winter snow, but weather forecasts cannot always predict just how severe a particular snowfall will be.

Severe winter weather causes a number of problems. In cities, the authorities have to pay the high costs of snow removal. Stock farmers in the north have extra costs for feeding their animals, while in remote farming hamlets some families may be cut off for days on end. In addition, Japan is occasionally subject to longer-term climatic difficulties. The following are the most common.

Drought

Rainfall in Japan is usually quite well distributed across the country and over the course of the year. As a rule, there is a balance (Fig. 2.20) between the amount of incoming precipitation and the moisture lost by evaporation plus transpiration from plants. However, in some years this balance may be disturbed and drought can then become a problem. This can come about in a number of ways:

(i) The *Bai-u* spell in early summer may produce less rain than normal.

(ii) The moving depressions which provide some of Japan's rainfall may in certain years edge past the country, without producing much precipitation.

(iii) The summer thunderstorms which are triggered off by local effects, such as hilly ridges, may also in certain years be less active than normal.

Cool summers

We have already seen that high temperatures are a basic feature of summer-time in Japan. Indeed, Japanese agriculture relies partly on sub-tropical crops such as rice, sweet potatoes and tea. Rice in particular is grown as far north as Hokkaido, where problems of summer climate can affect it. The difficulty is that both northern Honshu and Hokkaido sometimes have summers when monthly temperatures are two or three degrees below average. This happens when polar maritime air from the north persists until late summer. Poor rice harvests then follow, and in former times the result was famine.

3 The Seas Around Japan

Introduction

Japan is an island nation, and few Japanese live more than an hour's journey from the coast. Throughout the centuries, the sea has been an important factor in Japanese life. It influences the climate, offers opportunities for work in fishing and sea transport, and helps to keep Japan separate from neighbouring countries. The most obvious features of Japan's maritime situation are as follows:

1. The country is surrounded by deep ocean basins, separated from each other by even deeper ocean trenches. The shape of the ocean floor in turn influences the types of fish living in the waters surrounding Japan.

2. The country is also surrounded by a variety of ocean currents (see Fig. 2.13). From the south comes the Kuroshio, a broad, fast-flowing current of warm tropical water. As it approaches the southern tip of Japan, the current divides. One branch goes north-westwards, as the Tsushima current, while the other travels some way along the eastern side of the country, before heading out into the North Pacific. Both currents raise the temperature of the air by several degrees Centigrade, especially in winter. Meanwhile, from the north, the cold Oyashio current comes streaming past the island chain of the Kuriles. This chilly water cools the air surrounding eastern Hokkaido and north-eastern Honshu, which do not benefit from the warm Kuroshio. Ocean currents have other effects. Where contrasting cold and warm currents meet, as happens off north-eastern Japan, low cloud and fog are common. Again, typhoons which breed in the warm waters of the tropical Pacific move regularly towards Japan along the lines of the Kuroshio and Tsushima currents. While the ocean currents around Japan clearly affect the climate, they also create suitable living conditions for many species of fish.

Fishing

The seas surrounding Japan contain many bottom-living or *demersal* varieties of fish, such as cod, haddock and plaice. On the surface, meanwhile, there are several *pelagic* species, ranging from the large, such as the tuna, to the small, like the squid, mackerel and sardine. Although Japanese fishermen have been taking advantage of the sea's rich resources for centuries past, it was only after World War II that Japan became the world's leading nation in ocean fishing (Fig. 3.1).

Fig. 3.1 *The top six fishing nations (1976)*

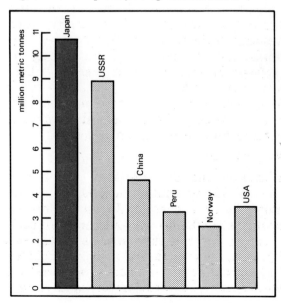

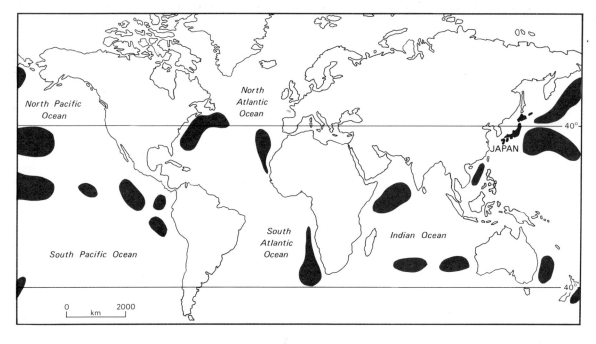

Fig. 3.2 *World areas fished by Japan*

Fig. 3.3 *Distant water fishing boats*

Today, we can recognise four main categories of fishery.

1. *Distant water*

This type of fishing is carried out by large boats, working far from Japan (see Fig. 3.3), and often remaining at sea for many weeks at a time.

2. *Offshore* fishing is done by small to medium-sized vessels, working within about a day's sailing from the Japanese coast.

3. *Coastal* fishing is done by even smaller craft, working within sight of the coast, and returning to port every day.

4. *Aquaculture*

Searching for fish in the open sea is always a rather risky and uncertain business. Hence, there has been increased interest in recent years in the farming of fish, shellfish and seaweed.

We can now look at these categories in turn.

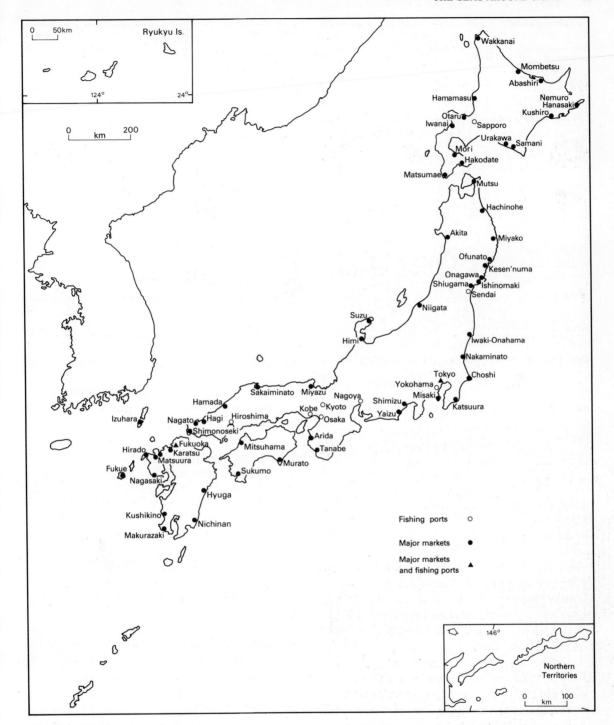

Fig. 3.4 *Fishing ports in Japan*

Distant water fishing

After several years of food shortage, during and immediately after World War II, Japan was eager for supplies of fresh food from the sea. By the 1960s, therefore, Japanese fishing boats were roaming the oceans of the world (Fig. 3.2), and all

Type of fishing	Size of vessel (tons)	% of total national catch	% by value	% of total employed
Coastal	under 10	39.2	29.2	81
Offshore	10 — 100	30.4	51.7	14
Distant water	over 100	30.4	19.1	4

Fig. 3.5 *Percentage of national catch taken by offshore, coastal and distant water boats (1980)*

through the 1970s Japan landed greater catches than did any other nation. One example of all this distant water activity is the tuna fishery of West Africa.

Far from their home ports of Shimonoseki and Nagasaki (Fig. 3.4), fleets of tuna boats, owned by large Japanese firms such as Taiyo Gyogyo Kaisha, fish off the west coast of Africa. A tuna fleet might consist of four boats, which operate in pairs. At sea, each pair tows a single large net which is then closed like a purse around a shoal of fish, trapping them in a wild flurry of foam. When the dripping net is slowly hauled in, the fish are immediately transferred to the large freezer ship which accompanies each fleet. There, the tuna are quickly processed and stored, until the holds are filled and the frozen cargo can be taken back to be sold in Japan.

The rest of the tuna fleet remains in the West African fishing grounds for some years. The port of Las Palmas in the Canary Islands is used as a base, where supplies of food, fresh water and fuel can be obtained, and where mechanical and electrical repairs can be carried out. Every few months, crew members are flown home to Japan, while others arrive to take their places. Other tuna fleets, belonging to the three main Japanese fishing companies, search the waters of the central Pacific. Using baited lines, fishermen toil long hours catching and hauling in tuna, which are then canned at factories on the islands of Western Samoa and Vanuatu, for example.

Changing requirements

Distant water fishing covers much more than the tuna catch, of course. Japanese trawlers, for example, scour the continental shelves of the North Pacific for cod, pollack and ocean perch. Others, meanwhile, fish for sardines in the cool Benguela current, off the coast of South-West Africa. All the time, however, changes are taking place in distant water fishing.

1. Fishing boats are becoming fewer in number. The use of machinery and electronic equipment on a large scale means that fewer seamen are needed. Yet in one sense this may be just as well, because young Japanese are nowadays not so keen to take jobs in deep-sea fishing.

2. Fuel costs have risen enormously since 1973. As a result, fishing companies have tended to reduce their more expensive distant water operations.

3. Problems of conservation have caused Japan to do less distant fishing, since the supplies of fish in certain areas have been so greatly reduced by unrestricted catching. Similar factors have affected Japanese whaling activities. The whale population in the Antarctic and North Pacific oceans has been so reduced by years of slaughter that it is no longer profitable for whaling fleets to hunt in these waters.

4. Since 1977, most maritime nations have established 200-mile zones, in which foreign fishing is restricted, around their coasts. Some Japanese fishing companies have been badly affected by this change.

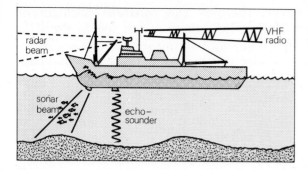

Fig. 3.6 *Modern aids to ocean fishing*

For instance, the fleets of crab boats, which used to sail northwards each year in large numbers towards Russian territorial waters, are now allowed only limited entry into that area.

Offshore and coastal fishing

Like their distant water counterparts, off-shore fishing vessels search for both demersal and pelagic species. Working inside Japan's own territorial waters, these vessels are usually smaller than distant water boats. However, as Fig. 3.5 shows, it is the offshore fishermen who provide the greater part of the annual Japanese catch.

An example of offshore activity is the mackerel fishery of the East China Sea, between Japan and South Korea. Mackerel, which swim in vast shoals numbering perhaps millions at a time, are trapped by purse seine nets, towed by fleets of six or seven boats. Each boat uses a series of modern devices (Fig. 3.6) to find the mackerel, first of all. Sonar beams, for example, can help locate shoals of fish, while echo-sounders plot the layout of the sea-bed below. Mackerel shoals prefer water with a mild temperature of about nine or ten degrees, and fishing boats therefore carry metering equipment to calculate the sea temperature. Finally, electric lamps are lowered to the sea surface to lure the fish towards the nets. Radar, meantime, enables the boats to identify surrounding objects, even at night or in fog, while VHF radio allows fishing boat captains to pass messages to each other. Eventually, when the nets are hauled in, the China Sea mackerel catch is taken to the Nagasaki fish market for sale.

Fishing for a living

Nagasaki, however, does not depend heavily on fishing for its existence. Yet many smaller settlements do. One example is the town of Choshi, on the coast to the north of Tokyo. At the fringe of Choshi are several villages, each with its own fishing fleet, on which many families rely for their livelihood. At Choshi Togawa, for example, there are over 200 vessels, some of which fish offshore, while the smaller ones work only in coastal waters. These coastal boats bring in shrimps and prawns, which are used mainly as bait by the larger vessels. Choshi owes its prominence as a fishing port to its location close to the zone where the Oyashio and Kuroshio currents converge.

Fishing cooperatives

As in most Japanese fishing villages, the busiest organisation in Choshi Togawa is the fishery cooperative. There are at least 2000 such cooperatives in Japan, and all of them work on similar principles. The cooperative provides a range of services (see Fig. 3.7) for its members, who in turn pay for these benefits. As Choshi Togawa, the cooperative actually does more than might be expected of the average fishery

Fig. 3.7 *Services provided by fishing cooperatives*

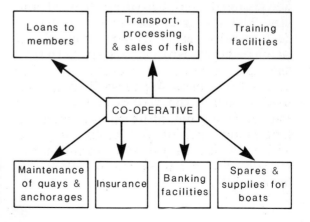

cooperative. It not only sends the daily catch direct to the central fish market in Tokyo, but it also maintains large storage tanks where surplus fish can be kept alive for a time. Not only does it supply its members with ice, new nets and machinery spares, but it also operates a radio station which keeps boats at sea in touch with their home base. Above all, the cooperative system helps its members to make a better living and gives them mutual protection when times are hard.

Referring back to Fig. 3.5, you will see that coastal activities are now the most profitable branch of Japanese fisheries. Distant water work, as we have seen, is restricted by several factors. To make up for this, more attention has also been paid in recent years to the farming of fish, shellfish and seaweed.

Farming the sea

Marine farming, or aquaculture, has been going on around the shores of Japan for several centuries, but over the past forty years it has increased tenfold. There are three important varieties of aquaculture.

1. Fish farming

The idea of hunting for fish across vast expanses of ocean seems very wasteful, when you realise that similar fish could be reared in sheltered bays and ponds, to be harvested when mature. In Japan, this idea has been successfully developed. Some fish farms grow salt-water species, like the yellowtail tuna and the sea bream (Fig. 3.8(b)). These are fed on smaller fish, such as sardines, or on low quality fish which could not easily be used in any other way.

Other species, like the eel, carp and rainbow trout, are kept in large freshwater ponds. Fish farms are more numerous in the warmer waters of southern Japan, but several farms have recently been developed further north, using the warm waste water from electricity generating stations. In every case, however, there is the constant problem of disease. Infections which would do little harm among fish in the open sea are likely to cause severe losses in the crowded conditions of a fish farm.

2. Shellfish

On the surface of Hiroshima Bay, large log rafts lie (Fig. 3.8a) anchored in rows. Beneath each raft, long lines dangle in the dark depths. Attached to each line are oysters, which filter nourishment out of the salt water. In winter, the lines are hauled out and the oysters are taken to nearby processing sheds, where the meat is separated from the shells. Refrigerated trucks then take some of the oyster harvest to shops and restaurants all over Japan, while the rest are canned.

Hiroshima Bay is just one oyster farming area. The coast north of Sendai is another, while the coast between Nagoya and Osaka is the world's main area for the cultivation of pearl oysters. In the same way, scallop shells are farmed in sheltered bays. On shore, shrimps are reared in large ponds, often on the sites of old coastal salt fields.

3. Seaweed

Although the Japanese eat only tiny amounts of seaweed at any one time, more seaweed is used each year in Japan than in any other country (Fig. 3.9). An example is the red algae, known as *nori*. This weed will only grow where it is submerged by the tide for most of the day, and is then exposed to the air for a few hours. Thus, *nori* farmers place heavy nets, supported at just the right height by bamboo poles, in shallow sheltered water, where the crop is harvested each winter. Until about 1960, *nori* cultivation went on close to the urban markets around Tokyo Bay. After that, increasing reclamation and pollution drove it outwards to less crowded parts of the Pacific coastline.

Fig. 3.8 *Aquaculture:* **(a)** *an oyster farm (above)*
(b) *a fish farm (below)*

Markets

Even though fishing and aquaculture employ less than 1% of the labour force and contribute less than 1% of the Gross National Product, it is an important industry for Japan because of the importance of fish in the Japanese diet (Fig. 3.10(a)). The link between these two facts is the business of fish wholesaling and retailing (Fig. 3.11). Japan's largest fish market is at Tokyo harbour, where hundreds of whole-sale agents deal with the daily landings of sea produce. Early each morning, shop owners arrive at the market to select their supplies for the day. Among the throng is, for example, one of the Komai brothers, whose fish shop in central Tokyo offers customers an enormous variety of seafoods. Water-thin slices of raw tuna are in constant demand, as are various kinds of shellfish from marine farms.

The Komai brothers also sell seaweed and cooked items, like deep-fried fish pieces and fish cakes. Most of the food on sale is traditional, but at least one new

trend is becoming clear during the 1980s. More and more of the seafood bought by Japanese households comes from aquaculture, rather than from conventional fishing.

Conservation

Japan's dependence on the sea for food leads to certain problems. For example, if any one species is over-exploited, then future catches will obviously decrease. Again, if industrial wastes and other poisons are allowed to damage the marine environment, the opportunities for fishing are likewise reduced. Conservation involves finding solutions to problems like these. In this section we can look at one important form of conservation – the use of regulations to control pollution.

Pollution control

The shallow waters along the Pacific coast of Japan were seriously polluted during the 1960s. While chemical and metal

Fig. 3.9 *Collecting seaweed by hand for processing locally*

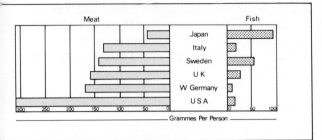

Fig. 3.10 *Fish as an element in the diet of selected countries. (Below) a serving of sushi for 2 or 3 people*

wastes were being discharged from coastal factories, household sewage and detergents were also pouring into these same waters. Fish die off quickly in such conditions, and would therefore not be used as food. Shellfish, however, can accumulate large amounts of metallic and other poisons, without necessarily dying. Then, when people eat those shellfish, the results can be disastrous (see Chapter Eight). To cut down the chances of human deaths from eating polluted seafood, Japan passed a series of laws, beginning in 1967 with the Basic Law for Environmental Pollution Control. This was followed in 1970 by the Marine Pollution Prevention Law.

Regulations like these have at least forced factory owners and others to take greater care before releasing dangerous wastes into coastal waters. In those areas where pollution problems were most severe, some improvement has appeared in recent years. Tokyo Bay, for example, was

Sushi

Fig. 3.11 *Local fish market*

at one time almost empty of fish, but by 1980 its muddy waters once again contained enough marine life to attract weekend fishermen.

The sea's other uses

Quite apart from fishing and fish farming, the seas around Japan have offered other opportunities. Sea water contains many minerals, and it was once common to find extensive saltpans along the coast, where sea water was evaporated, to leave salt behind. Coastal villages often made a living by exchanging their salt and fish for farming products from inland villages.

Valuable minerals

In modern times, more valuable minerals, like oils and gas, have attracted exploration rigs to the coastal waters of western Japan. Indeed, some people have argued that Japan should also try to make up its shortage of metal ore by searching areas of the Pacific Ocean floor which are known to contain nodules of metal, such as manganese. Again, Japan needs to look for renewable sources of energy (see Chapter Five), and the sea may some day be used for this purpose. During the 1970s, electricity produced from a specially designed vessel anchored in the Sea of Japan showed that wave power might be a possibility for the future.

Transport

Strangely, for a maritime nation, Japan for many centuries made only limited use of the surrounding seas for transport. However, during the last hundred years or so, Japan has built up a vast network of ship-borne overseas trade (see Chapter Ten) and also a complicated pattern of coastal traffic. For one thing, coastal ships carry essential supplies of fuel, food and fertilisers to the many small islands which fringe Japan, especially on its southern and western sides.

In addition, ferry services (Fig. 3.12) link each of the large seaside cities on the main island of Honshu with towns on the three lesser islands of Kyushu, Shikoku and Hokkaido. At the same time, the seas dividing the various islands of Japan act as a barrier to transport during severe winter weather, when ferry services are liable to delay. Hence, the government has spent considerable sums on building bridges and tunnels, to provide more reliable links between the islands.

Defence

The seas surrounding Japan have been a formidable barrier in keeping the country

Fig. 3.12 *Ferry terminal at Tokyo*

free from invaders. The result is that Japan, in the last thousand years at least, has had no waves of foreign immigration, in the way that so many other nations have had. During the earlier part of this century, Japan built up its naval forces, not only to keep out invaders but also to extend its own power over a wider area of the Pacific. However, the nation's defeat at the end of World War II saw the disappearance of the Imperial Japanese Navy. Since then, Japan has developed a Maritime Self Defence Force (Fig. 3.13), to protect its seas and coasts.

Japan's position, on the edge of Eastern Asia, means that it is in an area where the two world super-powers, Russia and the USA, confront each other (Fig. 3.14). Thus, Russian ships and submarines leaving the huge naval base at Vladivostok have to pass close to the Japanese coast in order to reach the ocean. Similarly, aircraft from Russian bases on the island of Sakhalin regularly fly along the edges of Japanese air space. Japan, in its turn, keeps constant radio and early warning radar watch over Russian activities. It also cooperates with the USA, by exchanging military information and by allowing America to use facilities at Japanese naval bases.

The sea, then, continues to mean many different things to the Japanese. It is a valuable source of food, a protection against possible invasion and a highway for trade.

Fig. 3.13 *Vessels of the Maritime Self-Defense Force (MSDF)*

Fig. 3.14 *Areas of military confrontation*

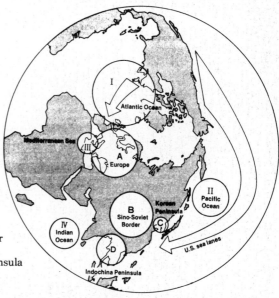

Ground and air forces
A: NATO forces and Warsaw Pact forces in Europe
B: Soviet and Chinese forces along the Sino-Soviet border
C: ROK and N. Korean forces on the Korean Peninsula
D: Chinese and Vietnamese forces on the Indochina Peninsula

Naval forces

I. The U.S. Atlantic Fleet (except the 6th Fleet and Mideast Force) and Soviet fleets (the Northern Fleet and Baltic Fleet) in the Atlantic Ocean.
II. U.S. Pacific fleets (centering on the 3rd and 7th fleets) and the Soviet Pacific Fleet in the Pacific Ocean.
III. The U.S. 6th Fleet and the Soviet Black Sea Fleet in the Mediterranean Sea.
IV. The U.S. 7th Fleet and Mideast Force and the Soviet Pacific Fleet in the India Ocean.

4 Making A Living From The Land

Main features

Knee-deep in mud, peasant farmers toil through the blazing heat of the day, planting row after row of rice seedlings. Without machinery and without chemical fertilisers, they labour patiently on. They have little choice, since their very livelihood depends on the harvest which will follow in six months time.

As a picture of Asian agriculture, this centuries-old scene is still true, for example, in much of India, Bangladesh, Burma and Indonesia. It is certainly not the case in Japan, although one can still see rice transplanting by hand, especially on small, traditional farms (Fig. 4.1(a)). In Japan, a number of factors have combined to produce a unique blend of East and West in farming. We can begin by examining three important features in this blend.

Intensive land use

Unlike most other nations, Japan has only a very limited area suitable for any form of farming. Because so much of the surface is mountainous, (steeply sloping) and heavily

Fig. 4.1(a) *Rice transplanting by hand*

forested, little more than sixteen per cent of Japan could possibly be cultivated. In one of the world's most densely populated countries, farmers respond to this scarcity of land in a number of different ways.

1. *Terracing*

As Fig. 4.2 shows, large steps can be dug out from sloping land. The flat fields formed in this way can then be irrigated.

2. *Irrigation*

Various crops, such as rice, produce a higher yield when extra water supplies are fed on to the growing plants. Since so many rivers run off the uplands of Japan, it has been possible to dig a vast maze of irrigation channels all over the coastal lowlands.

Fig. 4.2 *Terraces for cultivation*

Fig. 4.1(b) *Rice transplanting by machine*

3. Double crops and multiple crops

Many farmers in Japan, just like those elsewhere in Asia, plant one crop to ripen during the summer, followed by another winter crop in the same fields. In other cases, fields can produce two crops at the same time: fruit trees, say, along with dry-field cereals.

4. Arable rather than pasture

Pasture for farm animals does not usually bring the best possible returns from a given piece of land. Hence, Japanese farmers have always preferred crop growing to the rearing of livestock. Where animals are kept, they feed in stalls rather than take up valuable space in fields. The lack of pasture land also reflects severe climatic constraints on the growth of good-quality pasture grasses.

5. Small farms

Since space is so limited, most farming families in the past were only able to rent tiny plots of land. In 1947, when the laws governing land ownership were changed, tenant farmers were able to own fields which they had previously rented from landlords. Yet, the gains in size have not been very great, and the average farm is still little over one hectare (see Fig. 4.3). To make matters more difficult, even that small area is sometimes made up of several garden-sized plots, widely scattered.

6. High level of inputs

To make up for the fact that their farms

Fig. 4.4 *Rice plants showing grain heads*

are so small, the Japanese have always tried to apply the maximum input to the land, in order to get the maximum return. High inputs are achieved by putting in many man-hours of labour per hectare or by putting machinery to work wherever possible (Fig. 4.1b), by adding irrigation water and by using large quantities of weedkiller and chemical fertiliser. Over the years, the amount of labour has greatly decreased, while the inputs of machinery and chemicals have increased.

Rice: the dominant crop

As in most other Asian countries, there is one preferred food-grain in Japan. Rice (Fig. 4.4) has always taken up far more farmland than any other crop. In 1975, after years of decline, the planted area for rice still occupied 48 per cent of all the agricultural land in Japan; by 1981 it had dropped further to 41 per cent. Although rice can be grown in dry fields, almost all Japanese rice comes from fields which have been deliberately flooded. Over the past thousand years and more, therefore,

Fig. 4.3 *Farm size and farm population in selected countries (1977)*

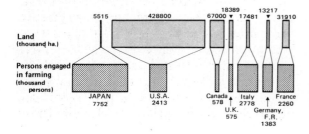

	1960	1970	1982
Overall self-sufficiency ratio	90	78	73
Cereals	82	45	33
Beans	44	13	9
Fruits	100	84	79
Vegetables	100	99	98
Milk and dairy products	89	89	85
Meat	91	89	80
Sugar	18	23	31

(%)

Source: Ministry of Agriculture, Forestry and Fisheries.

Fig. 4.5 *Changing self-sufficiency in food*

reservoirs and canals for irrigation have been constructed throughout the farmed lowlands. However, not only has rice-growing altered the landscape but it has also shaped the daily lives of people in farming villages.

Rice is a time-consuming crop to grow. Seedling plants have to be first raised in specially prepared beds of soil, before being taken out to be planted, row by row, in the fields. In due course, weeding has to be done, until the grain is ready to be harvested in autumn. To carry out these tasks efficiently, traditional communities in the Japanese countryside relied heavily on cooperation between farming families.

Rice has been dominant for a very long time, but it has been in steady decline since the late 1960s. For one thing, public tastes have changed, especially with regard to the widespread popularity of western-type dishes and 'fast' foods, such as hamburgers. The demand for rice has been going down by a small amount (about two per cent) each year. Yet, while this has happened, the quantity of rice grown per unit of area has kept increasing. The main reasons for these higher yields are the use of chemicals, good quality seeds and very close planting. As a result, production far exceeds public demand, and the Japanese government has therefore been forced to look for ways of reducing the surplus of rice.

Government influence

There are several reasons why the

Japanese government should be deeply concerned about agriculture.

1. National self-sufficiency

With a very large urban population, and a limited area of usable land, Japan has some difficulty in feeding itself. Hence, what the government has to ensure is that the country is as far as possible self-sufficient in most of its basic foodstuffs (see Fig. 4.5).

2. Farmers' votes

Whatever policy it adopts, the government cannot afford to clash frequently with farmers. Although most Japanese are now city dwellers, the countryside still retains the large share of political votes which it was given immediately after World War II.

3. Surplus rice

Running to over a million tons annually during the 1970s, the surplus of rice has proved an embarrassment to the Ministry of Agriculture, Forestry and Fisheries (MOAFF), especially since Japanese rice is so expensive to produce that no other country could afford to buy it.

The first two factors tend to outweigh the third, and thus government policies are on the whole generous towards farmers. For example, MOAFF officials meet farmers' representatives each year to agree on a national producers' price for the rice crop. This price is usually more than ordinary customers would be willing to pay, so the government then fixes a national consumers' price at a lower level, and makes up the difference to the farmers. However, to encourage rice farmers to switch to other crops, the government also offers bonus payments on a wide range of crops other than rice. Thus, if the market price for farm products like wheat, barley and soybeans should dip below an agreed minimum level, the government again pays the difference to the producer. In all, these

	Farm Households	Members of Farm Households	Cultivated Land	Cultivated Land per Household	Power Cultivators and Tractors	Dairy Cattle
	1 000	Millions	1 000 hectares	Ares	1 000	1 000
1967	5 500	28.6	5 938	108.0	3 079	1 376
1970	5 402	26.6	5 796	108.5	3 449	1 804
1974	5 081	24.1	5 615	110.5	3 714	1 752
1978	4 788	22.2	5 494	114.7	4 175	1 979
1983	4 522	20.8	5 411	119.7	4 405	2 098

Source: Ministry of Agricultue and Forestry.

Fig. 4.6 *Agricultural statistics: fewer farms but more machinery*

price policies are extremely expensive, although they do at least help Japan to be partly self-sufficient in food.

We have been considering some basic features of farming in Japan. Agriculture, however, does not remain static. So we also need to think about changing trends.

Changing trends

Overall decline

There was a time when Japan was a land of farmers. Until about a hundred years ago, manufacturing and service jobs occupied only a small minority of the population. That position has now been completely reversed. Farming has gone through a massive decline which shows clearly in the following ways.

1. *Decreased workforce*

The percentage of the workforce in agriculture has fallen dramatically. From a figure of 75 per cent in 1880, it went down gradually to 49 per cent in 1950 and then more rapidly to just 9 per cent in 1983.

2. *Part-time working*

The vast majority of adult workers living in the countryside now travel daily to work in some type of non-farm job. Much of the work done on farms is therefore carried out by retired people and house-wives.

3. *Falling share of national output*

Farming has a falling share in the total value of goods produced annually in Japan. In 1960, for instance, one-tenth of the Gross National Product GNP came from farming, but by 1975 the figure was down to one-twentieth.

The figures for rural decline (Fig. 4.6) are a little surprising, because conditions in the years after World War II were very favourable for farmers. The landlord system was abolished, tenants became owners and the growth of cities provided ready markets for farm produce. Yet these same towns and cities also offered job opportunities and steady wages for those rural dwellers who were willing to migrate or commute. Many were more than willing, and the outflow of people from the countryside became a torrent during the years 1965–75.

For small remote villages the results were quite disastrous. Fields were left unused, to become choked with weeds, while abandoned buildings mark where some elderly villager has died, with no close relative to take over the farmhouse. Villages decline in other ways. When the population falls below a certain level, there are no longer enough people to carry out shared tasks, such as road repairing or organising the summer festival. Again, with fewer residents fewer taxes are paid, and the local authority may even curtail some of the services which it provides.

However, it is only fair to point out that since 1975, there has been, a small counter-flow of population back to the

Fig. 4.7 *Tea-harvesting by machine*

countryside. Occasionally, villagers who have spent their working lives in large cities now choose to retire early to the family farm, where they can look after parents who are in their latter years.

Diversification

While decline has been affecting rural areas, those farmers who remain have been looking for ways of varying their output. Today, hardly anyone just grows rice. Some farmers have turned to livestock as a source of income, since the average Japanese consumer is far more willing to eat meat and drink milk now than in the past. Others have moved into fruit and vegetable production. The result is that in the 1980s the fields surrounding a typical village show a curious mixture of colours and textures.

Some of this variety is new, but some of it is not. For centuries, villagers in different parts of Japan have cultivated tea bushes (Fig. 4.7), groves of bamboo for use in fences and domestic utensils,

mulberry bushes for feeding silkworms and vegetables to accompany the daily diet of rice. Nowadays, variety is a key feature of Japanese farming.

Food imports

Having been a closed society for some 250 years up to 1868, Japan had to provide all its own food throughout this long period. Even up to the start of World War II, when the country had been open to western influence and contacts for 80 years, the pattern of self-sufficiency had not changed very much. It is only since 1945 that the Japanese taste has favoured foreign foodstuffs. As Fig. 4.8 shows, Japan by the 1970s had become heavily dependent on overseas supplies of food. Many Japanese, for instance, now eat bread as well as rice. The wheat flour needed for bread manufacture can be obtained far more cheaply from Canada and the USA than it ever could from local farms.

Again, Japanese farmers now keep

(%)

	Cereals	Pulses	Vegetables	Meat	Cow Milk and Milk Products	Fat & Oils
U.S.A.	162	142	99	97	93	181
France	170	69	93	92	110	51
Canada	183	79	68	100	97	91
Netherlands	30	8	195	189	195	27
Italy	73	99	118	76	74	50
Germany, F.R.	90	17	33	86	106	40
U.K.	77	81	79	71	83	17
Japan (1980)	33	7	97	81	86	29

Fig. 4.8 *International comparisons in food self-sufficiency (1978)*

large numbers of farm animals. Since there is hardly any room for animal pasture, stock farmers need to import huge quantities of maize and soybeans to feed their cattle, pigs and poultry. Finally, there is a public demand for various products, such as cane sugar, bananas and coffee beans, which usually grow in more tropical conditions than Japan can provide. The net result of these changes in food consumption is that Japan had by 1981 become the third largest food importer in the world.

Farm products

Despite the flight of people from the land, the rise in part-time farming and the drop in self-sufficiency, Japanese agriculture remains an important activity, employing over five million people. In this section, we will look at the three main groups of product which these farmers supply to the public.

1. Grains

For many centuries, the Japanese were a nation of farmers who grew rice as their main food. No other grain crop has ever occupied as much as a sixth of the area taken up by rice. But other cereals, such

as wheat and barley, were once quite widely grown, until competition from imported grain made them unprofitable. Since 1975, the government has been encouraging farmers to produce less rice, which is already over-plentiful, and to concentrate more on barley and wheat. Japanese wheat is soft and therefore not suitable for bread manufacture. Instead, it goes to make noodles, which feature regularly on Japanese menus. Barley, meanwhile, is used mainly in the manufacture of beer and whisky. The only other grain crop occupying large areas of farmland is maize, which is grown in northern Japan for feeding livestock and for human consumption.

In most countries, it is possible to map the major areas where different grain crops are produced. In Japan, however, this is not possible, because rice, barley and wheat are cultivated in countless patches nationwide, from Hokkaido in the north to Kyushu in the south.

2. Fruit and vegetables

While grain farming has been declining in recent years, the output from market gardens and orchards has been increasing (Fig. 4.9). Indeed, the area taken up by

	1960	1965	1970	1975	1980
Arable land (in 1,000 ha)	6,071	6,004	5,796	5,572	5,461
	(100)	(99)	(95)	(92)	(90)
Planted area (in 1,000 ha)	8,129	7,430	6,331	5,755	5,636
	(100)	(91)	(78)	(71)	(69)
Breakdown of planted area	100	100	100	100	100
Rice	41	44	46	48	42
Wheat, barley	19	13	8	3	6
Vegetables	8	9	11	11	11
Fruits	3	5	7	8	7
Mulberry trees	2	2	3	3	2
Feed and fertilizer crops	6	8	12	15	18
Others	21	19	13	12	14

Fig. 4.9 *Percentage of cultivated area in selected crops*

fruit growing expanded by four hundred per cent during the period 1947–72. When people are becoming wealthier as the Japanese were at that time, it is common for them to spend less money on cereal foods and more money on a variety of fruit and vegetables. In Japan, the most widely grown fruits are those shown in Fig. 4.10. Mandarin oranges, which do best on gentle slopes in areas with a mild winter, are restricted to the southern half of the country, while apples are produced only in the cooler northern half (Fig. 4.11). For many centuries, Japanese farmers have also grown mulberry leaves, for silk production, and tea, which is by tradition the national drink. Tea bushes appear on slopes all over central and southern Japan, where some farmers plant lines of these bushes as boundaries between fields.

Although the area of farmland planted in vegetables has been mainly static since 1975, the quantity produced per hectare has continued to rise. Japanese vegetable growers are among the world's heaviest users of chemical fertilisers and the use of labour-saving machinery also helps to raise productivity. In 1980, for example, over 90 per cent of all Japanese farmers owned small-sized cultivator-tractors. The outputs include crops such as lettuce, tomatoes, carrots and onions, which are familiar to western consumers. Japanese farmers also produce crops like water melon which require a sub-tropical environment. But, whatever their crop, vegetable farmers everywhere in Japan

Fig. 4.11 *Areas of fruit production*

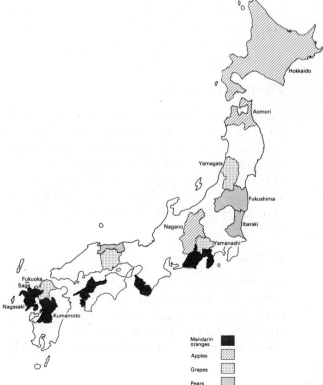

Fig. 4.10 *Changes in fruit growing, 1950–82 (1,000 ha)*

	1950	1975	1982
mandarin oranges	39 700	185 500	140 500
apples	34 000	53 200	53 100
grapes	4 400	29 200	29 600
peaches	4 600	17 200	16 300
pears	7 300	20 200	21 000
cherries	419	2 880	2 600
plums	7 600	16 300	16 200
chestnuts	9 500	44 300	43 500
mulberry	174 000	150 000	113 000

	Dairy cattle	Pigs	Poultry (000's)
1950	198 128	607 600	16 545
1960	823 500	1 917 600	54 627
1970	1 804 000	6 335 000	223 531
1983	2 098 000	10 273 000	307 063

Fig. 4.12 *Changing numbers of livestock*

are helped by local cooperatives, which enable members to share machinery, packing facilities and central heating for greenhouses.

3. *Livestock*

Until the late 1800s, there was little livestock on the average Japanese farm, although some oxen were kept for heavy work and horses were bred for military use. At the same time, the shortage of usable land meant that fields had to be sown with rice and other essential foods, rather than fodder or grass for animals. In addition, the Buddhist religion discouraged the eating of meat. However, in recent years there has been a very marked change (Fig. 4.12). A growing public demand for milk products and meat encouraged farmers to develop stock-rearing on a large scale, especially during the period between 1960 and 1970. Pigs and poultry, which can be kept indoors and so take up little space, fit fairly easily into the Japanese pattern of agriculture. Their main disadvantage is that their feedstuffs, such as grain and soybeans, have to be imported.

Dairy farms appear in two types of location. About half are on the outer fringe of large cities, to which milk is delivered daily, from cattle raised indoors on purchased feedstuffs. The remainder are in the cool northern provinces of Hokkaido (Fig. 4.13) and Tohoku, where they can spend part of the year on outdoors pasture. The milk from these farms goes to processing factories, to be turned into cheese, cream and flavoured drinks. Beef

Fig. 4.13 *Dairying in Hokkaido*

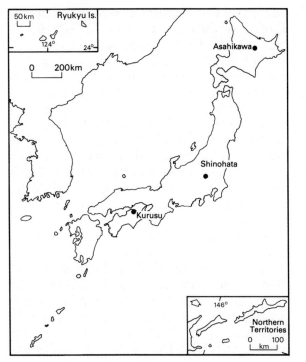

Fig. 4.14 *Location of three case studies*

cattle, which are just as numerous as dairy cattle, are concentrated in three main areas: the north, the central region of Kanto and the far south.

*   *   *

We have been looking here at the major sectors of Japanese agriculture. Yet it is important to remember that farms in Japan are run by millions of individuals, each with his or her own preferences and methods. The next section provides some details of three very different examples.

Modernised arable farming in northern Kanto

Keiji Yamamoto was born in 1950, in the village of Shinohata† where he still lives. Shinohata lies in the Isokawa† valley, surrounded by steep-forested hills, about 160 kilometres north of Tokyo (Fig. 4.14). When he took over the farm from his father, the four hectares of land produced rice, barley and vegetables. Keiji decided that that these crops needed too much manual labour, and he therefore turned to two specialties: sericulture and horticulture. Much of the land around Shinohata is too dry for irrigated rice, and Keiji has retained this crop in only one field of 0.2 hectares. Instead, he has gone in for mulberry production on a fairly large scale, as have many of his neighbours. Young leaves, cut regularly from the mulberry bushes (Fig. 4.15), are fed to silkworms which eventually make small white cocoons of fine silk thread. The silkworms are kept in long artifically-heated vinyl-covered sheds, which look very much like greenhouses. The silk itself is sold through the Shinohata Silkworm Rearers' Cooperative, which also helps to organise many of the tasks carried out jointly by its members.

Keiji has planned his farming system so that his activities are spread out over the year, and so that the drudgery of former times is reduced. He has therefore turned a third of his land over to horticulture, growing pot plants and ornamental bushes which customers buy for their homes and gardens. His own garden has been landscaped with rocks, shrubs and a pond, stocked with red and silver carp. Meanwhile, the large old farmhouse has been re-roofed, fitted with solar panels for water heating and with modern glass-and-aluminium sliding doors. All these are signs that Keiji Yamamoto has made a success of the farm which he inherited. Unlike some of his neighbours, he has not invested large sums of money in expensive, rarely-used machinery. Owning only a light truck and a power tiller, he leases other equipment from the cooperative. Keiji, in fact, is a careful businessman, representing the modern, well-organised type of Japanese farmer who has no need of any non-farm employment.

† Both are fictitious names. See Acknowledgements.

Part-time farmers of Shikoku

Koichi Sugiyama lives in the hamlet of Kurusu, where the coastal lowlands of Shikoku start rising to the mountainous interior of the island (Fig. 4.16). Like so many other rural families in Japan, the Sugiyamas and their ancestors have lived in the same village for at least two hundred years. Yet, Koichi, who is the present head of the household, may be among the last of his clan to farm in Kurusu.

The Sugiyama farm consists of just one hectare of land, divided into several small fields. In two of these irrigated rice is grown, in another cucumbers and in yet another table grapes. Six people live on the farm, but not one of them could be

Fig. 4.16 *A typical lowlands scene showing intensive farming using vinyl sheets*

Fig. 4.15 *Silkworm farming in Gumma Prefecture*

Fig. 4.17 *Potato harvest in Hokkaido*

described as a full-time farmer. Koichi's parents, both in their seventies, stay in the old homestead. Grandfather Sugiyama still potters around the fields, while his wife looks after the little flower and vegetable garden beside their house.

Meanwhile, the younger Sugiyamas (Koichi, his wife Tamako, their teenage son Ichiro and daughter Sadako) occupy a large new house nearby. Koichi works full-time as foreman for a construction company in the city of Takamatsu, about half an hour's drive from the farm. His wife is employed in a small factory which makes ski gloves. The factory is only a ten-minute walk from the Sugiyama home, and is itself typical of the many small businesses dotted about the densely peopled parts of the Japanese countryside. Whenever possible, husband and wife work on the farm at weekends and in the evenings. Yet, less than fifteen per cent of the total annual family income comes from agriculture. For the teenage Sugiyamas, farming seems to have little to offer. They attend high school, and usually manage to avoid helping on the farm because, they say, there is always school homework to be done. It looks as if they will both move off to urban jobs at some time in the future.

Dairying in Hokkaido

Norio Kirihata came originally from the island of Sakhalin, which once belonged to Japan. In 1945, when Russia claimed the island, the Kirihata family, including ten-year-old Norio, fled to Hokkaido, the nearest part of Japan. There they settled down to farm in the vicinity of Asahigawa City, in an area which was first colonised as recently as 1900. Farms in Hokkaido are far bigger than elsewhere in Japan, because the density of rural population is much less and demand is lower.

The Kirihata farm is even bigger than the Hokkaido average, since it was established on a block of land newly cleared

from forest only in 1947. Here, on their twenty hectares, the Kirihatas (father, mother and two sons) began getting used to the yearly cycle of cultivating rice, wheat, potatoes and sugar beet.

It was in 1970, following his father's death, that Norio took over the farm, just at the time when rice was reaching its peak of production in Japan. Since then, Norio's concern has been to make the maximum profit by diversifying his farming pattern. He has, for example, increased the land given over to root crops. The potatoes (Fig. 4.17) are now grown from high quality seed, to be marketed in the city of Sapporo, while the sugar beet is grown on contract to be processed in a nearby refinery.

The biggest change of all has been in livestock. Where his father kept horses to do some of the farm work, Norio has specialised in dairy cattle, and the milk output from his forty-two Friesian cows goes to a processing plant run by Snow Brand Products in Asahigawa. Dairy cattle require special feeding arrangements, and for this reason the Kirihata farm includes twelve hectares of hay and permanent pasture.

Yet this is not enough to feed the dairy herd in the severe climate of Hokkaido, where cattle must be kept

Fig. 4.18 *Main types of national land use*

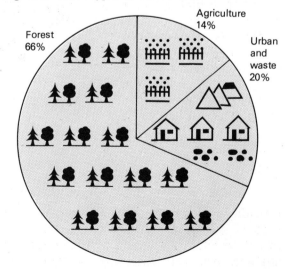

Forest 66%

Agriculture 14%

Urban and waste 20%

Fig. 4.19 *Softwood exploitation*

indoors for six months of the year. As a result, Norio needs extensive storage space for feedingstuffs, which he buys in, and large sheds for his cattle. Silos and cattle installations, neatly painted in white and red are distinctive features of the farm, which looks as if it belonged in Europe rather than Japan. Meanwhile, Norio looks ahead to the future with more confidence than Japanese farmers as a rule possess. His eldest son has done well at agricultural college in Honbetsu Town, and looks forward to the day when he in his turn can take over the farm.

Other land uses

Farming is by no means the largest user of land in Japan, as Fig. 4.18 shows. It is forest which covers most of the country's surface. For the Japanese of long ago, forests were a vital source of building material, tools and fuel, while in times of food shortage they provided valuable reserves of roots and berries.

Japan's forests are a mixture of deciduous hardwood, evergreen hardwood and evergreen softwood. Hardwoods, once used widely for charcoal and home construction, are no longer in demand; softwoods, by contrast, are (Fig. 4.19). Yet Japan is a major importer of both softwood for papermaking and hardwood for furniture, because local forestry has simply not been organised on a commercial basis.

In 1946, when the Land Reform Act was passed, the ownership of farmland was re-arranged, while forest ownership remained unchanged. Many medium-sized blocks of forest stayed in private hands, but were of limited use because of over-exploitation during World War II. Much of Japan's forested hill land is now covered by untidy natural re-growth,

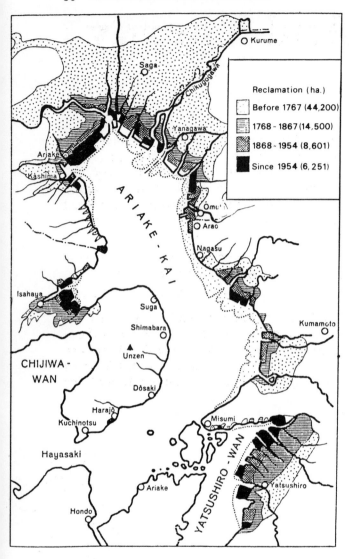

Fig. 4.20 *Land reclamation in Kyushu*

which has little value except to protect the slopes from erosion. At the same time, the Ministry of Agriculture, Forestry and Fisheries has been encouraging the re-afforestation of hill slopes with young conifers, but the benefit of these schemes will not appear until nearer the end of this century.

Since farming and forests between them take up four-fifths of the country, and since some of the rest is bare mountain, there is clearly very little space left to accommodate the human population. For many years now, Japan's lowlands have become ever more crowded, as cities grow outwards into the farmed areas. In many other countries, there is a clear contrast between rural and urban landscapes. Japan, once again, is different. Here, town and country merge into one another. The real contrast is between empty uplands, covered in forest, and lowlands, densely packed with farms, factories and towns.

In heavily populated countries, people sometimes look for ways of winning new land. The Dutch, for instance, have for centuries been reclaiming land from the sea. In Japan, large reclamation schemes have been carried out in Tohoku and Kyushu (Fig. 4.20), to produce new land for arable farming. Elsewhere, too, much time and effort has been invested in reclamation. However, as we shall see later (Chapter 12), most of this newly-won land is destined for urban-industrial rather than farming uses.

5 Minerals And Energy

Local minerals

Because metals are so important in modern society, an industrial nation like Japan needs large supplies of mineral ore, together with fuel for factories, homes and transport. Different metal ores occur in different types of physical region, as follows:

1. *Old crystalline rocks* contain ferrous ores, together with veins of non-ferrous ores, such as copper, lead and zinc.

2. *Sedimentary basins* contain useful rocks, such as limestone, and the main fuels (coal, oil and natural gas).

3. *Areas of surface deposits*, laid down by rivers or glaciers, contain sands and gravels, for example. Although Japan has each of these physical settings, it is mountain chains, made up largely of older metamorphic rocks and newer lavas, which dominate. As a result, non-ferrous metals are found widely throughout the country, while fuel deposits are not (see Fig. 5.1).

During the centuries when Japan was a closed society, ores were mined mostly on a modest scale, to be converted into metal in charcoal furnaces. Copper was a special case, being the only metal which could be described as plentiful. When Japan began to industrialise, demand for metals grew rapidly. Copper was now needed for electrical wiring, lead for electrical batteries and zinc for use in coating sheets of steel. Over the past thirty years, local mines have been unable to keep up with the demand, and in many cases the reserves of ore have now been mainly used up. Thus, by 1980 the mines shown in Fig. 5.1 were producing only six per cent of the copper required in Japan, while the

lead mines were meeting only about forty per cent of the requirements. In other cases, such as the aluminium industry, the ore needed does not occur at all in Japan. Imported metal ore, therefore, has a vital part to play in the Japanese economy.

Imported metals

Modern industry cannot exist without metals, and metals can only be made if ore supplies are readily available. Japanese companies, finding their domestic ores running short, have been quick to look for

Fig. 5.1 *Metal mining in Japan*

Major mining centre ●
Minor mining centre ·

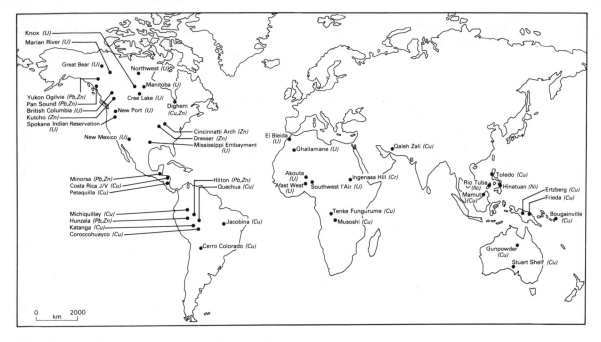

Fig. 5.2 *Overseas metal mining projects (1979)*

alternative sources. Fig. 5.2 shows that Europe and the USSR are the only regions of the world untouched by the Japanese search for metal ores. To ensure friendly relations with these overseas suppliers of ore, the Japanese have adopted various tactics:

1. *Offering loans* to underdeveloped but ore-rich countries. The Mitsubishi Corporation, for example, loans money to Papua New Guinea in return for steady supplies of copper from the giant Bougainville mine.

2. *Investing money* in joint ventures for the development of new mines in North and South America.

3. *Investing in overseas metal smelters*. Again, Mitsubishi has shares in aluminium projects in Queensland (Australia), Brazil and Indonesia. By importing finished metal rather than ore, the company gains an extra advantage. It is not consuming energy or creating pollution within Japan itself.

Of all the minerals which Japan lacks, iron ore is the most vital. The annual consumption is so vast that one company alone, Nippon Steel, takes in about 45 million tons annually. Of this total, about half is carried cheaply from Western Australia (Fig. 5.3) in gigantic ore carriers which discharge regularly at each of the company's six waterfront steelworks. However, Japan is not only short of metals. Energy has to be used to convert ore into metal, and the search for energy supplies has become an important topic in Japanese geography.

Energy

The Japanese are by no means the world's heaviest users of energy (see Fig. 5.4). They do, however, have a record of rapidly increasing demand. The total quantity of energy used in Japan during 1959 was doubled by 1965, and the 1965 total was doubled again by 1971. Then, after world oil prices rose sharply in 1973, the Japanese demand increased at a more modest rate. By 1980, Japan had become one of the few countries where the demand for energy was actually falling, although the economy as a whole was still growing.

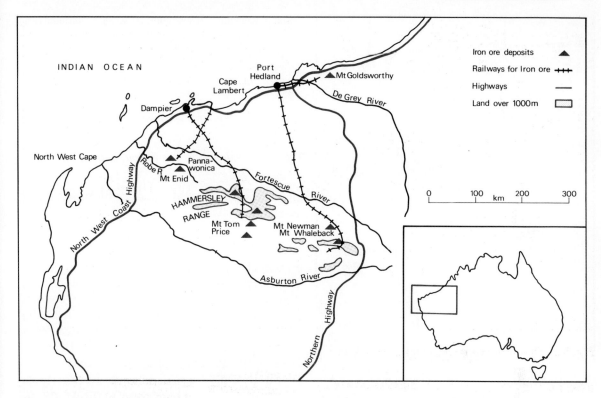

Fig. 5.3 *Iron ore mining developments in North-Western Australia*

Fig. 5.4 *Per capita use of energy in selected countries (1976)*

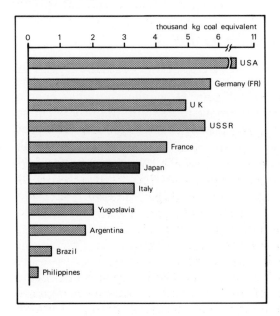

Behind these changes lie the energy policies of the Japanese government, which aims to reduce the total amount used and to reduce the over-dependence on imported oil. Thus, the balance between the major energy sources (Fig. 5.5) is constantly changing. We can now look at each of these sources in turn.

Fig. 5.5 *Main sources of energy*

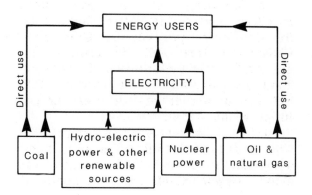

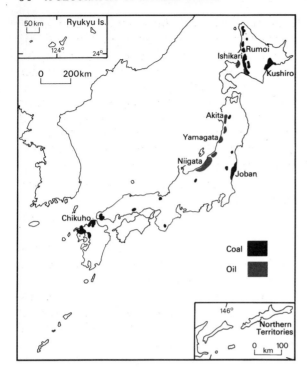

Fig. 5.6 *Coal and oil fields*

Year	Kyushu	Hokkaido	Honshu	National total
1930	20291	6727	4359	31376
1950	21374	11375	5710	38459
1960	26146	19043	7418	52607
1970	14750	19039	4540	38329
1980	7274	10736	85	18095

Declining output from Japanese coalfields, in thousands of tons.

Fig. 5.7 *Regional decline in coal mining*

Coal

In old Japan, the main fuel was charcoal, derived from wood. After 1870, in the early years of Japan's industrial revolution, machinery was often driven by river water. But charcoal and running water were not enough to meet the needs of large textile mills, metal smelters and shipyards. For that purpose, coal mining areas were soon being developed (Fig. 5.6). Of these, the Joban coalfield was exhausted first, and by 1975 the large Hokkaido and Kyushu fields were also working at a much reduced level (Fig. 5.7). Long before then, the best quality coal deposits had already been used up. Industry and power stations, the main users of coal, have therefore been forced to import most of their supplies. However, these users are mostly located on or very near the coast, and for them coal from overseas is just as convenient as domestic coal. During the 1980s, there are three important features

of Japanese coal use which deserve particular attention.

1. Local decline

From the peak production year of 1941, the output of Japanese coal has declined. The results, for scores of mining towns, have been extremely serious. As the number of coal miners has gone down from 370,000 in 1950 to only 20,000 in 1978, so those communities which depended entirely on mining have fallen on hard times. Surrounded by man-made mountains of pit waste, lacking decent amenities and offering poor job prospects for the young, these are forlorn and worn-out places. With people migrating out in large numbers, mining towns here resemble those of Western Europe. They are certainly not typical of Japan as a whole.

2. Increasing use

Both the production of coal and the demand for it were declining during the 1970s in Japan. However, there has been a recent increase in demand, mainly because the government has been concerned at Japan's excessive use of oil. By 1980, there were plans to double the amount of coal used for electricity generating over the next ten-year period (Fig. 5.8). This

Fig. 5.8 *Inputs to electricity generation*

	1973	1980	1990 (est.)
Oil	71.2	51.5	46.9
Coal	12.2	14.6	26.2
Gas	2.0	15.9	38.6
Nuclear	2.4	20.2	71.3
Hydro	17.6	23.1	36.0

Fig. 5.9 *Owase tanker terminal*

trend may cause problems of dust pollution and ash disposal, but such difficulties can be overcome.

3. *Dependence on overseas supplies*

An increase in the use of coal is possible only if cheap supplies are assured over a long period. With this in mind, the Japanese have made long-term agreements with coal producers in Canada and Australia. Mitsubishi, for instance, helped open up Australia's largest open-cast coalfield, in the Bowen Basin of Queensland. To keep down transport costs, coal is taken to Japanese ports by ultra-large bulk carriers. As coal has taken a greater role in the fuel economy of Japan, so the country has become by far the largest importer internationally (over 51 million tons in 1980). To the energy-conscious Japanese, a major advantage of coal over oil is that nothing is likely to cut off these essential imports.

Oil

Japan has small sedimentary basins (refer back to Fig. 5.6) on its west coast, around Akita and Niigata, where oil and natural gas have been exploited since last century. Yet this local supply is now of very little significance. During Japan's recovery from the destruction of World War II,

imported oil was the cheapest and most convenient source of energy. Throughout the 1960s, in fact, oil was unrivalled. As coal production dropped, the demand for oil grew by 500 per cent in ten years. Unlike its competitors, oil could be used directly as a fuel for transport and industry, or could be burned to produce electricity. The immediate results of this heavy reliance on oil were as follows:

1. The growth of new deepwater harbour facilities (see Fig. 5.9) to handle an annual intake of about 300 million tons of crude oil.

2. A growing demand for large tankers, all of them built in Japanese shipyards (see Fig. 6.18).

3. An enormous increase in oil refining capacity along the Pacific coast of Japan, with many types of chemical plants built next to the refineries.

4. An almost complete changeover to oil in the large new thermal power stations which were built alongside harbours, from Tokyo all the way south to Kitakyushu.

5. A nationwide network of main power lines, radiating out from these stations and providing electricity to small towns, villages and millions of rural homes.

The supremacy of oil turned out to be a temporary feature. During the 1970s, its position was weakened by a number of factors.

1. *Price rises*

The dramatic increases imposed in 1973 by the petroleum producing nations, and a further sharp increase in 1979, have caused problems for Japan. The price of oil affected many other costs, including food, plastics and transport, which the Japanese consumer has to pay. To keep up their living standards, wage earners looked for pay increases. Increased wage bills then left companies with lower profits and less money for new investment.

2. *Political instability*

The Japanese have been concerned that

Fig. 5.10   *Thermal power station*

much of their oil comes from the Middle East, where war and civil unrest are commonplace. Serious disturbances in Iran during 1978, for example, deprived Japan of a large amount of its annual supply of crude oil.

3. *Pollution*

The use of petroleum involves possible dangers of atmospheric and marine pollution. The latter could happen if a loaded supertanker were wrecked, releasing its cargo to damage wildlife and fisheries. Japan has fortunately escaped this menace. On the other hand, atmospheric pollution from refineries and oil-burning power stations (Fig. 5.10) has been very much a problem, as we shall see in Chapter 9.

Combined, these difficulties have pushed the Japanese government to decide in favour of alternative sources of energy (see Fig. 5.11). Yet it must be remembered that oil remains top of the energy table. In the waters off the west coast of Honshu, the search for oil goes on. Outside Japan, major companies such as Maruzen, Idemitsu and Mitsui actively explore for oil, from Alaska to South-East Asia. Beyond all that, Japan has another strategy: large-scale storage of imported oil. All main ports now have vast rows of silver-painted oil storage tanks, while at Kin Wan Bay on Okinawa is the world's biggest fuel storage facility. Together, these stores give Japan sufficient oil for 90 days, should outside supplies ever be cut off. Meanwhile, as other energy sources become more important, it is to nuclear power, the fastest growing of these alternatives, that we now turn.

Nuclear energy

Japan is the only country in the world to have experienced the effects of nuclear

	1973	1980	1990 (est.)	
Oil (direct)	67.1	65.1	58.6	mainly transport and industrial use
Coal (direct)	15.4	14.9	16.6	mainly industrial use
Gas (direct)	2.9	3.5	5.3	mainly household use.
Electricity	14.6	16.4	17.5	many uses
Other	0	0	2.1	mainly renewable! many uses.

Fig. 5.11 *Elements in total fuel consumption (1973-1990)*

war. Hence it is not surprising that the Japanese should be extremely sensitive towards any controversy about nuclear power and its uses. As Fig. 5.11 shows, most of Japan's energy is used directly for fuel in transport or in steelworks, for example. Electricity is a secondary or indirect form of energy, produced mainly by heating water to convert it into steam. So far in Japan, oil and coal have been used for this purpose. However, uranium rods can also produce the very high temperatures needed for large steam boilers.

Despite their reservations about the dangers of atomic radiation, the Japanese first became interested in this form of energy in 1956, when the Japan Atomic Energy Commission (JAEC) was formed. The search for suitable power station sites soon began, and two areas were eventually chosen. Both are coastal, since ocean water is the most economical means of cooling the equipment in large power stations. One area lies on the level, dune-lined stretch of coastline north of Tokyo, while the other is in Fukui Prefecture, on the opposite side of the country (Fig. 5.12). In each area, a group of atomic power stations has been built at a safe distance from major centres of population. A further advantage is that both areas are as stable as anyone is likely to find in earthquake-prone Japan.

The Japanese government, cooperating with private companies, set out on its nuclear development programme during the 1960s. By 1980, there were over twenty nuclear power plants in operation, and several more were due to enter service before 1990. Nuclear power thus plays an increasing part in the national pattern of electricity production. However, this

increase has not been free from difficulties, such as the following:

1. *Imported fuel*

The uranium which provides the radio-active heat used in power stations does not occur naturally in Japan. Hence there is the problem that the import of this essential material could be stopped if the policies of the supplier nations were to change. With this possibility in mind, Japan has signed long-term contracts with friendly suppliers, such as Canada, France and Australia.

Fig. 5.12 *Nuclear power developments on the Japan Sea coast*

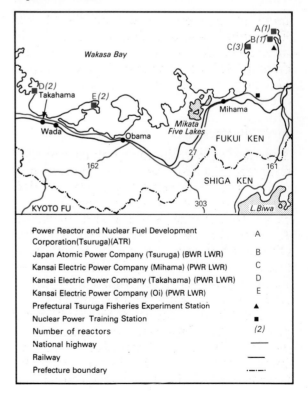

Power Reactor and Nuclear Fuel Development Corporation(Tsuruga)(ATR)	A
Japan Atomic Power Company (Tsuruga) (BWR LWR)	B
Kansai Electric Power Company (Mihama) (PWR LWR)	C
Kansai Electric Power Company (Takahama) (PWR LWR)	D
Kansai Electric Power Company (Oi) (PWR LWR)	E
Prefectural Tsuruga Fisheries Experiment Station	▲
Nuclear Power Training Station	■
Number of reactors	(2)
National highway	——
Railway	——
Prefecture boundary	·—·—·

2. Cost

Size for size, nuclear power stations are more expensive than any other type. In particular, very elaborate and costly safety precautions have to be taken. On the other hand, once a station is complete it does produce fairly cheap electricity.

3. Time

It takes years to prepare the site for a large nuclear power station. Then, very complex machinery has to be installed. As a result, it may take up to twenty years from the time a station is planned until it is actually ready to produce electricity. Meanwhile, over such a long period, public demand for energy may change in quite unexpected ways.

4. Safety factors

No other form of power production causes as much fear as does nuclear power. People living in the communities closest to a planned station have to be convinced that safety measures have been properly organised. So far, this has been done, and local opposition has not halted development, as it has done in Sweden and Austria, for instance.

5. Scarcity of sites

Nuclear stations need large open coastal sites, preferably far from existing towns and cities. Such sites are not easy to find in a land as crowded as Japan, and this factor will certainly limit future nuclear developments.

The combined effect of these factors has been to slow down the Japanese nuclear programme. Despite the advances made up to 1980, the share of Japan's electricity generated in nuclear power stations was less than had been originally forecast ten years earlier. Still, as more stations come into operation, it is clear that Japan ranks along with the USA and the UK as one of the nations most heavily involved in nuclear energy.

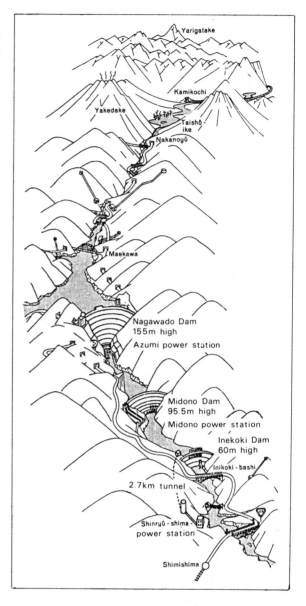

Fig. 5.13 *Hydro power developments in an Alpine valley*

Hydroelectric power

A country made up mostly of steep hills and mountains, with a heavy annual rainfall, seems to have ideal conditions for the development of hydroelectricity. Thus, when Japan began to industrialise, it was hydro power which supplied most of the electricity required. This situation continued until the early 1960s, when thermal power at last overtook hydro. By then, Japan had been divided up into nine regions, each with its own power authority responsible for distributing electricity within the region. These regions have quite unequal shares of hydroelectric development, which is heavily concentrated in the mountain ranges of central Honshu. The growth of hydroelectricity has in the long run been limited by a number of factors:

1. Small physical scale

Japan is not, by world standards, a large country. Hence its rivers do not have the extensive catchment areas needed to support hydroelectric schemes on the vast scale found in Canada or the USA. What has happened in Japan is that rivers have been harnessed to run hundreds of small electricity schemes. Fear of earthquake damage was another factor in the policy of not building massive concrete dams. Only in the 1960s, when hydro power was approaching its peak in Japan, were large schemes finally put into operation.

2. Limited number of sites

The most easily adapted and less remote sites are always the first to be used for hydroelectricity. By 1980, the majority of usable sites in the Japanese uplands had been put into use, and it is now inevitable that construction must ease off in the future. Some rivers, like the Azusa (Fig. 5.13), have been completely transformed by a long series of dams.

3. Seasonal irregularities

Ideally, the water supply in an electricity scheme should not vary much in quantity from one season to another. Japan is fairly fortunate in this respect, but winter can be a difficult time, when snow and ice cover the catchment basins of the upland hydroelectricity schemes.

These are some of the drawbacks which together ensure that hydro power is now only a modest element in the national supply of power. At the same time, it is fair to recall that hydroelectricity has brought some special advantages to remote parts of central Honshu.

1. Rural electrification

Hydro schemes are often constructed in rather isolated rural areas, where no other type of electricity may be available. In these circumstances, hydroelectricity is extremely useful in providing power for farms, homes and small factories.

2. Multi-purpose uses

Dams and man-made storage lakes on upland rivers can be used for more than power production alone. For example, they can control floods, while supplying irrigation water for agriculture.

3. Tourism

Road building has accompanied the construction of hydroelectric schemes in the central uplands. As a result, tourists can now drive alongside the storage lakes, between high forested slopes. However, the minor benefits which tourism brings are perhaps outweighed by the problem of depopulation. Local people have been migrating out along the same roads which bring the visitors in, and many upland districts lost about a quarter of their population during the period 1960–80.

On a lesser scale than hydroelectricity are several alternative forms of energy. Japan has been experimenting with power derived from wind-driven propellors, wave-driven turbines and solar panels. However, none of these has yet made a

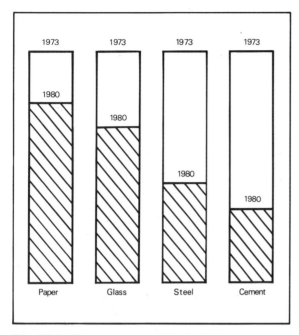

Fig. 5.14 *Energy conservation in industry, 1973 and 80*

significant contribution. On the other hand, geothermal power, derived from steam which has been created by volcanic activity, is already in use.

Conservation

Energy questions are of prime importance in Japan. Finding stable long-term sources of imported fuel is one vital concern. Another is the development of renewable sources. Coal, oil, natural gas and nuclear energy are after all non-renewable, and some time in the future when these sources are exhausted Japan will have to look elsewhere. Geothermal, hydro, solar, wind and wave power are all able to harness natural sources of energy which will last indefinitely. For that reason, the Japanese government pays for research into each of these alternative sources. However, another essential strategy is the conservation of energy.

Japan has been using a variety of methods in recent years to promote energy conservation. In 1980, the New Energy Development Organisation was set up to consider ways of using alternative energy sources, which would help reduce the dependence on imported oil. That is not all. In any advanced nation, private cars use a sizable fraction of the country's liquid fuel. To reduce this, the Japanese have passed strict laws, requiring cars to have pollution-free engines. At the same time, the government subsidises public transport, encouraging commuters to travel by train instead of by private car. Meanwhile, many industrial firms have appointed energy conservation managers.

By careful monitoring of the use of energy, and by using alternative sources where possible, the industries shown in Fig. 5.14 have reduced their consumption of precious oil. Other conservation strategies include an annual Energy Conservation Day, to help increase public awareness. In all, Japan has fully recognised its national problems, such as the lack of domestic resources, and has energetically searched for solutions.

6 Industry

Introduction

At his home outside London a young building society cashier is getting ready to leave for work. Glancing at the breakfast time programme on television (Sanyo), he puts on his wrist watch (Seiko) before going out to the car (Nissan). At work he has on his desk a video display unit (Nippon Electric) and an electronic calculator (Sharp). During his lunch break, he leaves the office to buy colour film (Fuji) for his camera (Canon), and a blank tape (Sony) for use in his car stereo system (Toshiba).

Quite clearly, not everyone in Britain owns as many Japanese-made goods as this young man does. All the same, most British homes do have at least one item carrying the imprint *Made in Japan*. Yet this is not really surprising, since Japan is a world leader in several types of manufactured product. This chapter will ask you to think about some of the factors which have helped Japan to reach its present high status as an industrial producer.

Basic features

In some ways Japanese industry is similar to industry in any other advanced country. However, it also shows features which are not commonly found anywhere else.

1. *Late start*

While European countries were busily developing factories of all kinds during the first half of the 1800s, Japan was still an isolated nation of farmers, warriors and shopkeepers. However, after 1868, when Japan was opened up to foreigners and their ideas, modern industries began to grow, using methods which had already been tried out in Europe and America. Over the following hundred years, Japan set out to catch up with the western industrial nations. With government support and with little competition from imported goods, the Japanese have eventually achieved their aim. Japan's late start may have been a disadvantage at first, but having learned from the mistakes of others Japan is now in a position to give industrial lessons to its rivals.

2. *Organisation*

Like other industrial nations, Japan has a

Fig. 6.1 *Percentage of industrial employees in firms of different sizes (1981)*

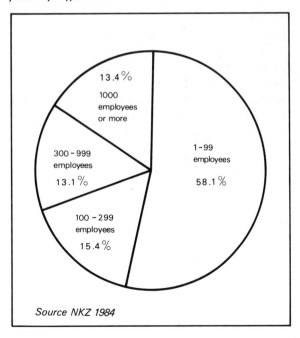

13.4%
1000 employees or more

1-99 employees
58.1%

300-999 employees
13.1%

100-299 employees
15.4%

Source NKZ 1984

	1960	1970	1979
Japan	17.4	18.1	20.0
West Germany	15.0	14.6	12.8
France	—	16.7	17.8
UK	7.1	8.8	14.3
USA	5.0	7.5	5.8

Source: *U.S. Department of Commerce & OECD*

Fig. 6.2 *Personal savings as a percentage of income in selected countries*

mixture of firms of different sizes. At one extreme is the small two-man workshop which is part of a family home. At the opposite end of the scale are vast steel works, covering hundreds of hectares and employing several thousand people. What is unique about Japan is the very important part played by small and medium-sized firms (see Fig. 6.1). Not only do they employ a majority of the huge Japanese industrial labour force (13.8 million in 1981), but they are also vital in two other ways. For one thing, it is often smaller firms which supply large manufacturers with essential parts. A car assembly plant, for example, would depend upon many sub-contractors for items such as wing mirrors, windscreen wipers and brake linings. In addition, it is smaller firms which dominate the craft sector of Japanese industry, producing pottery, traditional clothing and household furniture.

3. *Human relations*

Japanese industry has a system of human relations which is not widespread in other countries. Everyone seems to realise that each company has to operate as a team. Workers do not try to obstruct their own managers, who are in turn inclined to think carefully about the welfare and feelings of their workers. The larger firms demand high productivity from each employee, but in return offer numerous benefits, such as job security, company housing where needed, holidays at company hotels and large wage bonuses paid twice yearly. Meanwhile, in the many small firms, where working conditions are poorer and wages are are generally lower,

it is the bond of family relations which makes individuals loyal to the firm.

Throughout Japanese industry there is a constant search for methods of improving quality and lowering the production costs of each article made. Managers and workers see these as shared aims, and it is this joint determination which helps to make Japanese companies such strong international competitors.

4. *Wages • Savings • Investment*

It can be difficult for any manufacturing company to keep on raising the wages of its employees, unless the company's products are earning an ever greater income. Throughout the industrial nations of the West, countless conflicts have arisen over this problem. In Japan, by contrast, wage rises are usually tied to increases in output per worker. If modest wage increases are one advantage for Japanese firms, the large amounts of money saved by individuals (Fig. 6.2) are an advantage for the country as a whole.

Savings can be put to work, and this is usually done through reinvestment. No other country puts as much of its annual earnings back into new equipment (Fig. 6.3). As a result, Japanese industry tends to be more efficient than its rivals. Yet there are disadvantages in putting so much money into industrial investment. Housing, for instance, has not received much attention and neither have urban amenities, such as parks or playgrounds.

5. *Cooperation between government and industry*

Long-term planning· is something which

Fig. 6.3 *Investment in capital equipment as a percentage of GNP*

	Average	1976	1978
Japan	34.9	31.0	30.2
West Germany	24.9	20.6	21.5
France	23.8	23.2	21.4
UK	19.1	18.9	18.0
Italy	20.9	20.1	18.8
USA	18.8	16.4	18.0

Source: *Union Bank of Switzerland & IMF*

	1960	1970	1977	% 1981
United Kingdom	15	16	24	30.0
Germany	16	19	23	29.5
Japan	9	9	12	15.1
USA	4	4	6	9.7

Source: OECD Trade Statistics, Series A and E

Fig. 6.4 *Dependency on export sales in selected countries*

all successful industrial firms must do. In Japan, the government has not left companies to do all their own planning. Instead, the Ministry of International Trade and Industry (MITI) has cooperated with manufacturers, advising them and in some cases financing research into new developments. This sort of partnership between industry and government has worked more easily in Japan than it could do among the western nations. One reason is that Japanese companies have been traditionally ready to do whatever is best for Japan. Another reason is that government policy is not likely to change following an election, as might be the case in France, Britain or America. Since 1955, only one political party, the Liberal Democrats, has held power in Japan.

6. Large domestic and overseas sales

Japan, as we noted earlier, produces goods which are sold all over the world. Yet all those Japanese firms whose names are now household words in other countries began by selling goods in the home market. Japan, with its unique language and culture, and its relative isolation on the edge of Asia, has not been an easy market for imported products. This means that home-based industries have been free to sell their cars, radios, calculators and watches to the huge local population, before turning their attention to overseas customers.

Chapter 10 considers the importance of overseas trade to Japan, but for the moment we must stress that home sales are absolutely vital for Japanese firms. Fig. 6.4 shows that exports are much less important for the Japanese than for many other nations.

7. Disadvantages

Despite what we have been saying, it would be quite wrong to think that Japanese industry is always successful. There are failures and problems here, just as there are in every other country. For the present, we can consider just three of the difficulties which Japanese industry has to face.

(i) Shortages of raw materials and fuels. These are shown in more detail in Chapters 5 and 10.

(ii) Declining sectors. Some industries in Japan are too expensive to run, for one reason or another. Aluminium smelting, for example, requires too much costly electricity. In 1979, aluminium produced in Japan was fourteen per cent dearer than aluminium imported from Canada, where electricity is very much cheaper. The textile industry, on the other hand, has declined because labour costs in Japan are far higher than in the newly industrialised countries of Hong Kong, South Korea, Singapore and Taiwan, which now export textiles to Japan.

(iii) Trade barriers. A number of governments, worried by the flood of Japanese manufactures entering their countries, have begun to restrict imports from Japan. The Japanese are responding by setting up branch factories in foreign countries, from which the profits will still come back to Japan.

Industrial trends

Many of the changes which are now taking place in Japanese industry are intended to solve the problems mentioned above. Among the most important recent trends are high-value production, overseas investment and regional relocation.

1. High-value production

During the years of recovery after World War II, Japan concentrated first on industries requiring large numbers of workers

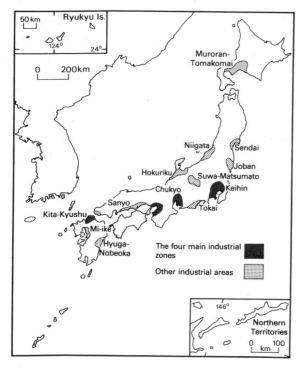

Fig. 6.5 *Industrial regions*

and fairly simple machinery. Clothing, toys, food processing and metal smelting were examples. Later on, the emphasis moved to assembly industries, such as cars and shipbuilding, where a large investment in equipment is needed.

More recently still, the government has been putting its faith and its money in those industries which are most likely to succeed during the closing years of the twentieth century. Among these is information technology. Computer manufacturers like Fujitsu, Hitachi and NEC are typical of firms which depend on advanced scientific knowledge, high productivity and high value of output.

Research is always essential to these firms, and in this case government assistance is especially useful. Not only does it provide finance but it also supports the training of scientists and technologists (Fig. 6.6). Robotics is another type of industry to which the Japanese have given particular attention. More and more factories are run on automatic lines, with robots doing the boring tasks which

people once did.

2. *Overseas investment*

Japanese companies have been investing steadily in overseas ventures. In some cases they do so to take advantage of a supply of raw materials. The Mitsubishi Corporation, for example, runs pulp, paper and sawmills in Canada, using local timber. The same firm owns aluminium smelters in Brazil, Indonesia and Australia, where there are vast supplies of bauxite ore. In other cases, overseas investment takes advantage of the low costs of local labour. Thus, Mitsubishi has also invested in textile mills in Taiwan and Thailand. Yet another reason for foreign investment is the need to overcome the trade barriers mentioned earlier. While the government of a European country might, for example, ban the import of Japanese television sets, it would be less likely to ban Japanese firms from investing in television assembly in that country.

3. *Regional relocation*

As Fig. 6.5 shows, much of Japanese industry is concentrated in the three major urban areas of Keihin, Chukyo and Hanshin. Ever since 1960, efforts have been made to attract industry to areas outside these main city-regions. However, as we will see in Chapter 12, the relocation of industry has taken place rather slowly.

Fig. 6.6 *National output of graduates on arts, science and engineering in selected countries*

		Total	*Science*	*Engineering*
Japan	1970	240,921	7,209	48,481
	1984	372,247	12,234	70,486
U.S.A.	1970	877,676	81,956	52,434
	1979	999,548		
U.K.	1970	97,359	24,516	16,422
	1980	104,992	19,924	15,279
France	1970	49,564		+ agr. 12,753
	1978	65,285		11,362
West Germany	1970	38,164	2,840	3,820
	1981	93,993	5,763	6,285

The Location of industry

Manufacturing industry in Japan exists to make profits. Money is invested in factory buildings and machinery. The individual people and companies who invest their money will always expect to get back more then they have put in. To achieve the expected profits, industrial firms usually follow two basic rules. First, they try to produce their goods at the *lowest possible cost* to themselves. Next, they try to sell the finished goods at the *highest possible price*. The first is often easier to achieve than the second, and firms can do so in the following ways.

(i) The firm can choose to operate in an area where its *raw materials* are easily available.

(ii) The firm can choose a location where the whole *process of production* can be carried out in the cheapest possible way.

(iii) The firm might place its factory so that it is as close as possible to its main *markets*.

Each of these aims can be difficult to achieve, but to achieve all three at the same time is virtually impossible. As a result, most Japanese factories are located in places which offer some sort of compromise between the three main choices. Here are some examples.

Raw materials locations

Certain raw materials which are needed in industry are bulky or awkward to carry. Among these, as Fig. 6.7 suggests, are timber and sulphur. Other raw materials, like fresh milk, soft fruit and vegetables, are perishable and cannot be transported over any great distance. In all these cases, the industries concerned are usually found close to the raw materials which they need. Thus, the first modern pulp and paper mills were opened in Hokkaido, close to Japan's main forests of softwood (Fig. 6.8). Similarly, canning factories for oranges are built close to the main orchard areas of the south and east. However, since most of Japan's raw materials have to be imported, it is at the ports where these materials are discharged that most processing is done.

Locations with low production costs

If Japanese factories cannot often locate close to their raw materials, they have equal difficulty finding places where the cost of manufacturing can be kept down. One possibility would be to build factories wherever energy is easily available, but Japan offers few such opportunities. Another approach is to locate where average wages are low. In labour-intensive industries, requiring many workers, the annual wage bill makes up a large part of each firm's total costs. Hence, during the 1950s, textile weaving moved out from its established centres of Osaka, Nagoya and Kyoto, to expand on the west coast where wages were then lower.

Market locations

Some industries find that the most profitable type of location is close to their markets. Examples include book publishing and various branches of food manufacture. As we have already seen, some kinds of food processing occur in the areas which grow the raw materials, such as sugar beet or mandarin oranges. But if the end product itself is bulky or perishable, then the food manufacturer will tend to locate where the markets are. Hence, meat packing, baking, cooking oil pro-

Fig. 6.7 *Industries and their raw materials*

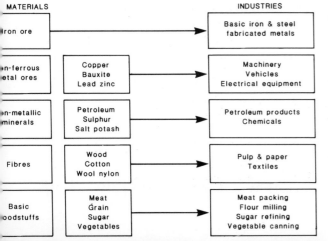

MATERIALS		INDUSTRIES
Iron ore		Basic iron & steel fabricated metals
Non-ferrous metal ores	Copper Bauxite Lead zinc	Machinery Vehicles Electrical equipment
Non-metallic minerals	Petroleum Sulphur Salt potash	Petroleum products Chemicals
Fibres	Wood Cotton Wool nylon	Pulp & paper Textiles
Basic foodstuffs	Meat Grain Sugar Vegetables	Meat packing Flour milling Sugar refining Vegetable canning

Fig. 6.8 *Softwood forest in Hokkaido*

duction and soft drinks bottling are all found around the major cities of Tokyo, Yokohama, Kobe, Osaka and Nagoya.

The national pattern

Japan's 13.8 million industrial workers are distributed throughout each of the forty-seven prefectures which make up the country. However, the distribution is highly uneven, as Fig. 6.9 illustrates. Between them, the four biggest industrial regions have for many years produced about half the total national output of manufactured goods. At the heart of each major region is a large city: Tokyo in Keihin, Osaka in Hanshin, Nagoya in Chukyo and Fukuoka in Northern Kyushu. Of these, the first three already had countless craft workshops, centuries before modern industry ever arrived from

the West. Outside these regions, newer areas of industry have been growing since 1950, to make up one of the world's greatest manufacturing zones – the Pacific Coastal Belt (see Fig. 1.15)

Keihin

The city of Tokyo had a population of a million people in 1850, when Japan was still a closed society. Such a huge market would demand food, cosmetics, furniture and metal goods, amongst other things. Today, the Tokyo market is many times

Fig. 6.9 *Percentage of national output from major industrial regions*

Region	1955	1974	1981
Keihin	21.5	18.6	17.6
Hanshin	20.1	16.3	14.0
Chukyo	10.8	11.1	11.8
N. Kyushu	4.9	2.7	2.7
Tokai	4.0	4.2	4.5

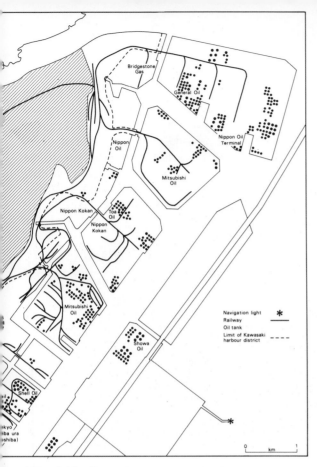

Fig. 6.10 *Coastal industry in the Kawasaki area of Tokyo Bay, 1980*

tractors. Then, all around the shores of Tokyo Bay, but particularly on the south side, is a series of huge industrial plants. Here, occupying reclaimed land and depending very much on imported raw materials, there are steel mills, petroleum refineries and shipyards. Fig. 6.10 shows just one small corner of these coastal flats.

Over the entire Keihin industrial region, an outstanding trend in the post-war period has been the gradual decline in inner city activity and the growth of manufacturing in the outlying prefectures adjacent to Tokyo. Yet, in the past five years (since the late 1970s), the number of small-scale manufacturing establishments has begun to rise again in the 'inner-city' areas of Tokyo, Osaka and Nagoya.

Hanshin

The enormous industrial area of Osaka-Kobe is only slightly less productive than Keihin. It, too, has many thousands of small workshops, making an endless variety of small consumer goods such as spectacles, pencils, matches and umbrellas. What gives Hanshin an advantage is that it was the first part of Japan to set up industry along modern western lines. In particular, metal smelting and cotton textiles were expanding here as early as the 1870s. The latter is now in decline, but Hanshin still has a third of the major steelworks in Japan.

During this century, extensive reclaimed areas, just like those in Keihin, have been constructed along the Hanshin coastline. Steel mills, marine engineering works, food processing plants and petrochemicals works have quickly taken up all this newly-won space. Inland, on the north side of Osaka, is a series of factories which make household electrical equipment. Their names are recognised almost everywhere in the world: National Panasonic and Sanyo, for example. Beyond that again, a mass of separate towns, each with its own industrial output, makes up the outer edge of the Hanshin manufacturing region.

greater and requires a truly vast industrial output to supply its wants. Looking out across Tokyo from the windows of a high-rise hotel, your first impression is of a fantastic maze of homes, factories, roads and railways stretching further than the eye can see. The fact is that Tokyo's industrial pattern is a highly-intricate mixture, in more ways than one. Not only do factories mingle with houses, but so also do large factories with small, old with new and heavy manufacturing with light.

Yet behind all this there is a kind of order. In the inner city are those activities which can operate in a restricted space. Printing and publishing make up one major branch of industry here, along with various small-scale manufactures such as briefcases, pens and jewellery. Further out are hundreds of assembly plants, putting together cameras, machine tools and electrical machinery from a variety of parts supplied by thousands of small sub-con-

Chukyo

The third main industrial region in Japan is smaller than than Keihin or Hanshin, and lies midway between these two. Its core is the city of Nagoya, but it extends into the adjoining prefectures of Aichi, Mie and Gifu (see Fig. 6.11). As we shall see in more detail later, this area makes a major contribution to the Japanese car industry. In some ways, the Chukyo region resembles its larger neighbours. Like them, it has reclaimed coastal land, where huge tonnages of imported raw materials, including crude oil, coal and metal ores, are converted into semi-finished products such as steel and chemicals. Like Keihin and Hanshin, Chukyo also has a great number of small workshops (16,924 in 1975), employing fewer than twenty

Fig. 6.11 *Nagoya and its surroundings*

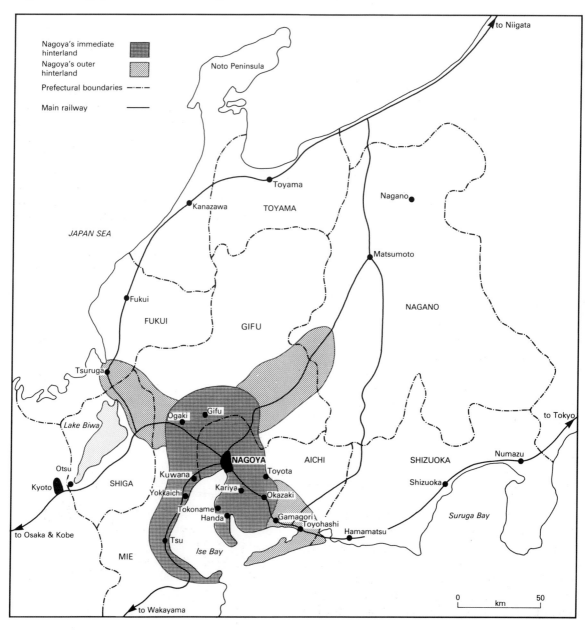

Fig. 6.12 *Tokai industry (paper-making)*

employers, and among its modern successes are piano and motor cycle assembly. Tokai is the home of notable firms such as Honda, Suzuki and Yamaha. Again, a third medium-sized industrial region, based on steel, chemicals and paper making, has been growing up in the northern island of Hokkaido.

Having seen the overall pattern of manufacturing in Japan, we can now look more closely at the distribution of some of the country's biggest industries.

The steel industry

1980 was the year in which Japan, after years of steady growth, finally overtook the United States as the leading steel producer in the non-Communist world. Yet the industry had quite humble beginnings in Japan. Steel is made from iron, which is in turn smelted from a mixture of coke, iron ore and limestone. Thus, the Japanese iron and steel industry began

Fig. 6.13 *Distribution of main steel plants (1980)*

people each. Some make traditional goods, like pottery or furniture, while others produce parts for bicycles, cars and office machinery. By contrast, large firms with over a thousand employees each are few in number (240 in 1975).

Northern Kyushu and the lesser industrial regions

Northern Kyushu differs from the three leading regions. It is rather newer, contains less variety and has suffered a considerable recent decline. Steel making has been a major employer here since the 1920s, followed by chemicals and food processing. However, while this area has been running into difficulties, others have been more successful. Referring back to Fig. 6.5 you will see that three particular areas stand out. The long coastal region of Setouchi, which stretches between Hanshin and Northern Kyushu, has developed its own steel mills, car assembly plants and petroleum refineries. Farmland and fishing villages have meanwhile disappeared under the spread of manufacturing.

Between Chukyo and Keihin, yet another coastal region has become industrially more productive. Tokai takes in about 150 kilometres of coast, including the cities of Hamamatsu, Shizuoka and Numazu. Its food processing and paper-making factories (Fig. 6.12) are major

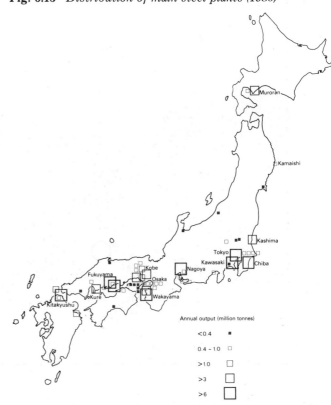

Annual output (million tonnes)

<0.4

0.4 - 1.0

>1.0

>3

>6

Plant	Country	Projected capacity
		Million metric tons
Fukuyama	Japan	16
Kashima	Japan	15
Kimitsu	Japan	14
Yawata	Japan	12
Oita	Japan	12
Chiba	Japan	10
Kakogawa	Japan	10
Mizushima	Japan	10
FOS	France	10
Taranto	Italy	10
Wakayama	Japan	9
Dunkirk	France	8
Nagoya	Japan	8
Hoogovens	Netherlands	6
Tabarao	Brazil	6
Pohang	Korea	6
Burns Harbor	USA	6

Source: Magazines and Hout

Fig. 6.14 *World's major deepwater steel plants (early 1980s)*

around Kamaishi, where ore existed, and around Kitakyushu, where coking coal and limestone were available. Since then, its distribution (Fig. 6.13) has been mainly governed by the fact that Japan has limited reserves of coal and almost none of iron ore (see Chapter Five). Supplies,

therefore, have to come in by sea, and all modern Japanese steelworks are built on the waterfront.

In recent years, Japan has been able to draw on coal from Canada, Australia and the USA, and on ore from Australia, India and Latin America. In many of these sources of raw materials it is Japanese investment which has helped development to go ahead.

Five major firms dominate the industry, and each of them has built enormous steelworks (see Fig. 6.14), to take advantage of the economies achieved by large-scale working. These massive works also profit from concentration, whereby everything needed is located on the one site. Sea-borne raw materials come in to one side of these works (Fig. 6.15), and finished steel leaves from the other side. None of the major steelworks is more than 100 kilometres from a main city, and all have nearby markets in industries such as shipbuilding, car assembly and electrical engineering. Since modern Japanese steel manufacturers can produce high

Fig. 6.15 *NKK steel works at Fukuyama*

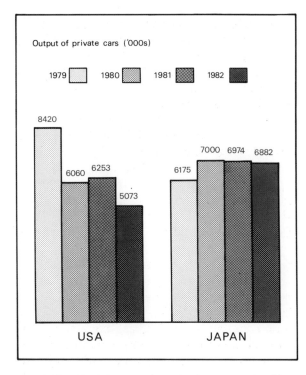

Output of private cars ('000s)

1979 · 1980 · 1981 · 1982

USA · JAPAN

Fig. 6.16 *Changing output of private cars in the USA and Japan (1978-80)*

quality goods at a competitive price, they have also been able to sell all over the world. North Sea oil and gas pipelines, for instance, are made largely from Japanese steel.

Car manufacture

One of the most remarkable of Japan's industrial successes is car making. In 1958, the country produced 188,000 vehicles, but by 1970 it was assembling 5.3 million. Its major firms, Toyota and Nissan, are now among the world's leading vehicle manufacturers, while in 1980 Japan itself emerged top of the international vehicle table (see Fig. 6.16). This success is based on a number of factors. For one thing, Japanese car plants are large and use automation wherever possible. Productivity per worker is extremely high: in 1980 45 vehicles per worker, compared with only 15 per worker in Western Europe.

Each major car firm concentrates on economical medium and small-sized models, and is thus able to find markets readily in a world of costly petrol. However, complaints about the flood of imported Japanese cars have been voiced in Britain and America, for example. To offset this, the Japanese have been building branch factories in several overseas countries.

The distribution of the car industry in Japan is tied to the major industrial regions of Keihin, Chukyo and to a lesser extent Hanshin. These are the most important markets and also the most convenient areas for the assembly of various parts from hundreds of sub-contractors' workshops. We can look at the city of Toyota to see how vital the car industry can be for particular districts.

The Toyota family were manufacturers of machinery for the textile industry until 1936, when they first branched out into the assembly of vehicles. Since the 1950s, the company has expanded greatly, in and around Toyota City. They control several factories (Fig. 6.17.) Since employee welfare is always important for large Japanese companies, Toyota also control thousands of flats and dormitories for their workers. The company also owns hotels, medical clinics and sports facilities. Since it pays most of the taxes raised in the district, Toyota has a considerable influence in local politics as well as in the economy. In return, the local authority has offered cheap land and an efficient infrastructure, including roads, a rail link and water supplies.

Shipbuilding

Like car manufacture, shipbuilding in Japan grew quickly in the years 1952–77. The government gave it priority assistance and with initial advantages of low-cost labour and cheap steel Japan was soon supplying half the world's annual

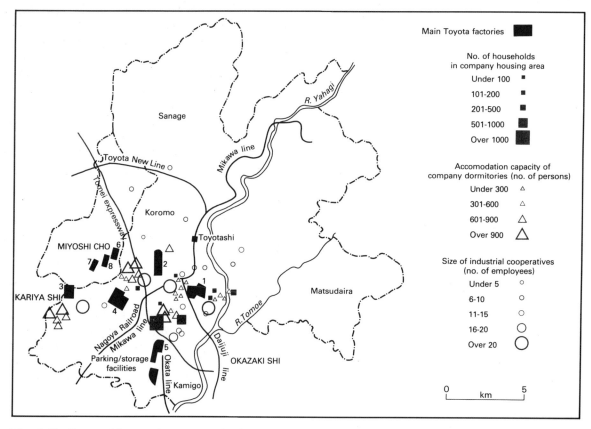

Fig. 6.17 *Toyota Motors: factories and other facilities (1976)*

tonnage of new ships. More recently, the success of this industry has been due more to the use of very advanced technology (Fig. 6.20) which, as in car manufacture, enables the well-paid labour force to be extremely productive. In addition, Japanese shipyards concentrated for many years on the construction of the largest size of tankers (Fig. 6.18), and thereby achieved economies of scale.

The industry has a small number of very large yards, and many hundreds of smaller enterprises. Each of the main shipyards (Fig. 6.19) is part of an industrial corporation producing a great deal more than ships alone. Mitsubishi Heavy Industry, for instance, is the biggest builder of ships in Japan, and it is also involved in constructing chemical plants, aircraft, electrical power systems and refrigeration equipment. An important advantage of this variety was that after 1977, when Japanese shipbuilding began to decline, the firms concerned could shift their attention from ships to other products.

The location of shipbuilding is partly

Fig. 6.18 *The increasing size of tankers built in Japanese shipyards between 1952 and 1977*

When built	Ship's name	Tonnage (DW/T)		Where built
1952	Petro Kure		38,042 dw/t	NBC-Kure
1954	Phoenix		46,526 dw/t	NBC-Kure
1955	Sinclair Petrolore		56,089 dw/t	NBC-Kure
1956	Universe Leader		85,515 dw/t	NBC-Kure
1959	Universe Apporo		114,360 dw/t	NBC-Kure
1962	Nissho Maru		132,334 dw/t	Sasebo Heavy Ind.
1966	Tokyo Maru		153,687 dw/t	Ishikawajima-Harima Heavy Ind.
1966	Idemitsu Maru		209,413 dw/t	Ishikawajima-Harima Heavy Ind.
1968	Universe Kuwait		326,898 dw/t	Mitsubishi Heavy Ind.
1971	Nisseki Maru		484,377 dw/t	Ishikawajima-Harima Heavy Ind.
1973	Globtik Tokyo		483,664 dw/t	Ishikawajima-Harima Heavy Ind. Kure
1974	Nissei Maru		372,400 dw/t	Ishikawajima-Harima Heavy Ind. Kure
1975	Homerice		447,000 dw/t	Ishikawajima-Harima Heavy Ind.
1976	Esso Deutschland		421,000 dw/t	Kawasaki Heavy Ind
1977	Esso Atlantic		500,000 dw/t	tachi Zosen Ariake

Fig. 6.19 *Distribution of shipyards in Japan (1980)*

related to the major industrial regions which we discussed earlier. The main grouping surrounds the Inland Sea, which has traditionally been a vital maritime highway. Recently, Northern Kyushu has been the only area to show any signs of expansion. Kyushu has a relatively mild winter, allowing shipbuilding to go on unhindered by weather. It also has rather more space than the overcrowded cities further north, plus a supply of local labour which is now unobtainable elsewhere.

During its years of unrivalled supremacy, the Japanese shipbuilding industry used to supply the world market. With low prices and regular delivery times, the Japanese had little difficulty in beating their Western European competitors. Since 1976–77, however, a group of new shipbuilding nations, including Spain, Brazil, Taiwan and South Korea, have seriously challenged Japan. The result is that shipbuilding is now one of the few depressed sectors of Japanese industry.

Fig. 6.20 *Mitsui Engineering and Shipbuilding Co. works at Chiba, Chiba Prefecture*

Electrical assembly

While the shipbuilding industry has lost ground, car and steel making have also probably passed the peak of growth. By contrast, the electrical industry in Japan has experienced a hundred years of continuing expansion, although its products have changed radically over that period. One of the earlier lines was the manufacture of power equipment, such as generators and transformers. In this field, one example is Hitachi Engineering, which located its factory at the small town of Hitachi, north of Tokyo, in 1907. Since then, the town and the company have grown out of all recognition, but the standard pattern of a one-industry town is as obvious here as at Toyota City. Hitachi supply employment, housing and shopping facilities for most of the population. Even the electricity, gas and water systems are operated by the company. The employees, for their part, supply the expertise and hard work which helps Hitachi products to sell internationally.

Like Hitachi, Mitsubishi Electric is a leader in the Japanese electrical industry. Success in this area depends firstly on anticipating how demand is likely to change in the next few years, and secondly on mass producing reliable goods. Mitsubishi's enormous annual output can be classed in four groups: *consumer goods*, such as electric fans, air-conditioning and microwave ovens; *industrial goods*, including motors and power tools; *heavy equipment*, for use in ships and power stations; and *electronic products* (see Fig. 6.21). The last named are of special

Fig. 6.21 *Ultra-high-voltage electron microscope, designed and built in Japan*

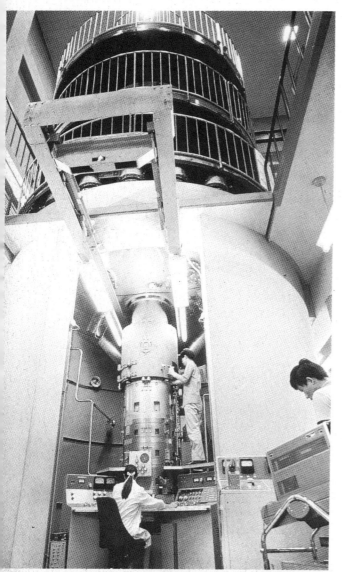

Fig. 6.22 *Average number of hours required to assemble a 20" colour TV set (1977)*

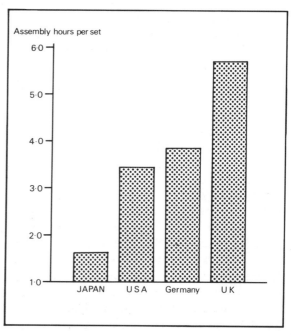

importance during the 1980s, and among them are space satellites, radar and microcomputers. In this case, the Japanese government has assisted by paying up to a third of the research costs and also by discouraging Japanese customers from buying foreign computers.

Equally, the government has kept foreign computer manufacturers out of Japan. This sort of protection has helped firms like Mitsubishi to grow to their present size. By 1981, the company had 42 centres of activity in Japan, and another 67 overseas, ranging from Calcutta, Mexico City and Singapore to Haddington in Scotland. In every Japanese industry which competes on a worldwide scale, as we have already explained, high productivity and attention to detail are essential elements. As Fig. 6.22 suggests, the electrical industry is well able to hold its own.

Craft industries

The four examples which we have been considering are all basically modern. There is, however, another sector of Japanese manufacturing which has existed for well over a thousand years. Crafts, such as handcarving of wood or domestic paper-making, were once common throughout Europe, but were in most cases driven out by modern production methods. In Japan, on the other hand, the old endures along-side the new (Fig. 6.23), because the Japanese have held on to a number of ancient fashions in clothing, diet and house furnishings.

Every large town has at least one area where such articles are still made. Many Japanese brides, for instance, wear tradi-tional embroidered silk gowns (*kimono*) on their wedding day. Again, floors in Japanese homes are usually covered with thick straw matting (*tatami*) made in family workshops in Tokyo, Osaka and Kyoto. Of all the major cities, Kyoto is the

one which has clung most strongly to older ways, and it remains a centre for making furniture, lacquerware, baskets and bamboo curtains, among many other craft skills. Japanese tastes in food and drink also allow scope for long-established crafts like the making of *saké* (rice wine) or of wooden utensils for the tea ceremony.

Among Japanese crafts, paper manu-facture has a special place. Made from tree bark, hand-crafted paper is used for in-ternal screens in homes, and as wrapping for gifts. At religious festivals, paper

Fig. 6.23 *Shoji Hamada — Japan's most famous twentieth-century potter*

lanterns are still widely used, while many people own paper fans or umbrellas made from strong water-resistant paper. However, as mechanised papermaking, based on softwood pulp, has increased all through this century, the craft side has steadily declined.

Conclusion

Japanese industry is unique, not only in its mixture of very old and very new, or of very small and very large. It is also unique in its success. No other country has such a gap between the huge quantities of manufactured goods exported and the small amounts imported. Japan has been able to avoid what is known as *advanced country disease*, whereby strong trade unions fight for feeble industries, kept going in a form of living death by taxpayers' money.

Likewise, Japan has been careful never to export any product which has not first been tested in its own home market.

Industrial prosperity is not simply a matter of having a strong domestic market. It requires a large measure of agreement between government ministries and businessmen. Furthermore, it requires employees who are determined that their firm should do well, and customers who prefer to buy Japanese-made goods whenever possible. All of these factors are present in modern Japan. Last but not least, the choice of a coastal location for most of the heavy industries has proved a clear advantage. Raw materials are discharged at the spot where they will be processed into finished goods, which can then move easily to their destinations, either by land or sea.

7 Services

Introduction

Jobs in agriculture help to keep Japan supplied with food, while manufacturing industry provides the clothes, cars and other possessions which people use in their everyday lives. Yet it is not in industry or in agriculture that most people work. As Fig. 7.1 shows, the percentage of employees in tertiary work is very much more than the combined percentage in primary and secondary.

In recent years, the numbers employed in service jobs have increased steadily. While machinery can take over much of the hard work in farming and manufacturing, there are still a great many service tasks which cannot yet be easily automated. The public might be unhappy, for example, if passenger aircraft were flown with no aircrew, or if medical operations were carried out by machines.

In Japan, customers still like to be served by shop assistants, while parents of school children still prefer lessons to be taught by teachers rather than by robots. It is true that many routine office tasks can be handled very well by machines, but services as a whole continue to employ over thirty million workers in Japan.

Retail and wholesale	17.0%
Professional services	8.5%
Transport	6.5%
Personal services	6.0%
Finance, insurance, real estate	3.8%
Central Government services	3.8%
Business services	2.2%
Repair services	1.3%

Fig. 7.2 *Nine main categories of service employment, with percentages in each category, 1978*

Classifying services

Service employment covers a vast range of jobs, as Fig. 7.2 illustrates. It is easier to analyse these jobs if we first arrange them into groups, such as the nine which are shown. However, not all services can be easily fitted into any one category. Computer programmers, for example, work in banking (a financial service), in the Ministry of Finance (a government service) and in the offices of industrial firms (a business service). The next section will look at the major categories of service, of which wholesale and retail is by far the largest and most widespread.

Wholesale and retail

Wholesale and retail services (Fig. 7.3) between them keep the Japanese public

Fig. 7.1 *Percentages of employees in primary, secondary and tertiary categories, 1900-1981*

	1900	1920	1950	1962	1971	1981
Primary	70.0	53.8	48.5	30.1	17.3	10.2
Secondary	13.8	20.5	21.8	31.1	35.5	34.7
Tertiary	16.2	23.7	29.6	38.7	47.2	55.1

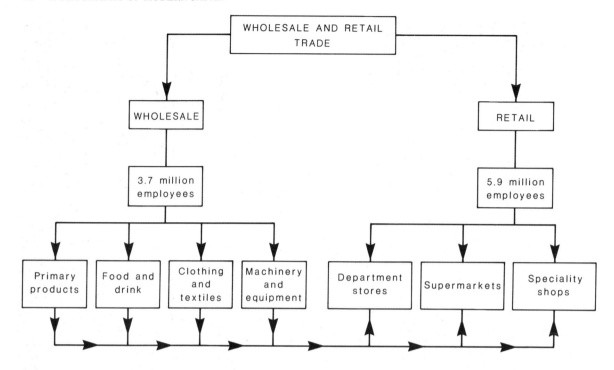

Fig. 7.3 *Classification of wholesale and retail services*

supplied with the essentials of life. In one way, Japan resembles other advanced countries. Manufacturers produce the goods which consumers want. These goods are bought by wholesalers, to be stored and passed on to retail traders, who sell directly to the consumer. But there are other ways in which Japan is different.

1. *Numerous small establishments*

About two-thirds of all Japanese shops are tiny, employing only one or two people.

Fig. 7.4 *Local family shops*

The majority of these small businesses sell food, and they exist in such large numbers because of two Japanese traditions. The first is the custom of buying fresh food every day, rather than storing the weekly shopping in a large fridge-freezer, as often happens in western countries. Second, there is the common habit of going out for snacks and drinks, instead of preparing every meal at home.

2. *Importance of wholesaling*

Wholesale firms are more numerous in Japan than in any other country. There is on average one wholesaler for every 300 people, whereas in Britain there is only one for every 1000 of the population. Yet, the existence of so many small shops, with no transport of their own and nowhere to store bulk supplies, means that wholesale firms have an essential part to play in the Japanese economy.

3. *Generally low efficiency*

While Japanese industry has adopted all

Fig. 7.5 *Modern luxury shops*

kinds of up-to-date techniques, the same cannot be said for the wholesale and retail trade. Small businesses, although open for long hours, do not usually sell enough in a day to make large profits. Their goods are therefore expensive. In addition, goods are generally expensive because they pass through the hands of several middlemen, on the way from the manufacturer to the customer. At the same time, the Japanese do not see the inefficiency of their small shops as a serious national problem. Manufacturing industry, which must face international competition, needs to be highly efficient. Retailing and wholesaling do not, since they face no foreign competition. If anything, the very complicated system of distributing goods helps to dis-

courage foreign imports from the Japanese market.

Competing with the small shops which are found all over the towns and cities of Japan (Fig. 7.4), there are two other types of retailer. One is the super-market, selling food, textiles and household items, while the other is the department store, which offers all sorts of goods under one roof.

Case study

Daibu Tokita is external sales manager of the huge Matsuzakaya store in central Tokyo. His job is to sell goods to customers by telephone calls and by personal visits, and he has a staff of 100

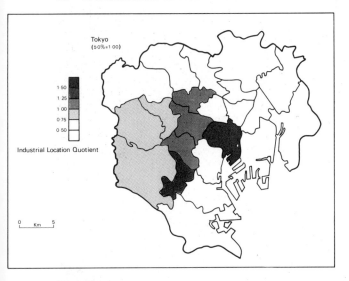

Fig. 7.6 *Districts of Tokyo, showing the central concentration of employment in financial services*

sales and clerical assistants to help him do this. This sort of service, unusual outside Japan, caters mainly for high-income clients. As Japan has become one of the world's great trading nations, so some of its citizens have been able to afford very expensive luxury goods (Fig. 7.5). Some of these goods are locally produced, while others are imported.

In the last year, for example, Mr Tokita has personally taken groups of customers specially to buy traditional silks made in Kyoto and pearls from the Shima district. Meanwhile, an outing to buy diamonds meant a return flight to far-off Belgium. The job, he insists, involves much pressure. On the one hand, he has to keep careful track of the performance of each of his sales personnel. On the other, he has to meet the monthly sales targets which the company directors set for his team. However, like many Japanese salesmen, Daibu Tokita enjoys both the challenge of his work and also the comfortable life-style which his salary allows.

Financial services

Western nations employ many people in insurance offices, banks, loan companies and estate agencies. Until recently in Japan these opportunities existed only on a small scale. During the 1960s, however, major changes took place. As the Japanese economy grew quickly, industrial companies looked for ever larger loans from banks, while more wage-earners could afford to take out insurance policies. Credit agencies also grew, as at least some Japanese gave up the old national habit of paying for purchases only in cash. By 1978, as a result, about four per cent of the entire workforce were in financial services, and the proportion continued to grow as Tokyo became one of the world's major banking centres.

High order financial services tend to look for central sites in the largest cities (Fig. 7.6). There, they are accessible to the maximum number of customers and also to each other. Where financial services cluster together, they occupy buildings which are easy to identify. Thus, the Marunouchi district in central Tokyo (Fig. 7.7), with its banking headquarters and offices for fire, vehicle and life insurance, is unique in Japan. Nearby, too, is the Tokyo Stock Exchange, which is of particular importance in a country where one person in every six owns stocks and shares.

Although Tokyo is dominant, other cities do have their own share of financial services. There are, for instance, stock exchanges in Osaka and Nagoya, and every smaller city has its own central grouping of savings banks, insurance offices and credit associations. Meanwhile; employment growth in this sector is likely to stop, as more and more of the tedious clerical work is done by computers.

Business services

The manufacture and marketing of goods require a great deal of organisation. Every large Japanese firm must have a head office, where accounts and records are kept and plans are made for the future. Most companies locate their headquarters in the central business district of one of

Fig. 7.7 *The Marunouchi business district in central Tokyo*

the three largest cities. Central sites are desirable because they have prestige and because they are close to the main railway terminals which bring commuting employees to and from work.

In the field of business services, some of the biggest employers are the trading companies, such as Mitsui, Mitsubishi and Sumitomo, which have long been an important element in the economic life of Japan. A trading company buys and sells goods all over the world, and so has to deal with raw materials suppliers, manufacturers, financiers and government departments. To make profits from international trading, it is vital for these companies to store vast amounts of up-to-date information about the prices of goods, transport costs and foreign exchange rates.

Mitsui, for example, operates banks,

chains of supermarkets and centres for the distribution of goods, all of which need service employees. In the company's main offices in Japan (Fig. 7.8) there are thousands of business service jobs, ranging from senior managers to junior clerks. Into these offices, hundreds of telex messages flood in through every hour of the day and night, to be analysed by economists and computer experts.

On a typical day, the Mitsui head office may arrange for turbines to be sent from the United States to a new power plant in Indonesia, or for lengths of heavy steel piping to go from Antwerp to a drainage project in Venezuela. At the same time, Mitsui might be buying thousands of tons of American grain for export to Greece, managing pepper plantations in Brazil, and cooperating with British Petroleum to exploit natural gas in the Arabian Gulf. Imagine all these arrangements repeated for many different goods in many different countries (Fig. 7.9), and you will begin to see how complex is the working of a modern Japanese trading company.

Fig. 7.8 *Location of Mitsui offices in Japan*

Fig. 7.9 *Location of Mitsui worldwide investments (1980)*

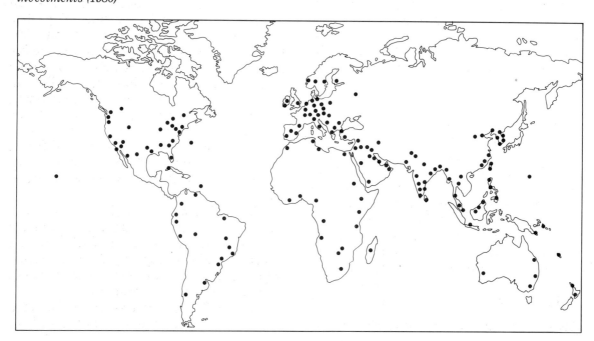

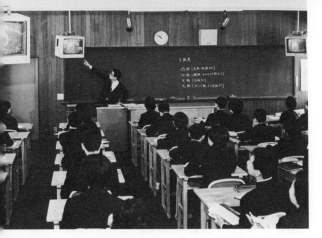

Fig. 7.10 *Inside a Japanese classroom*

	Total public sector
Japan	12.9%
West Germany	20.6
France	21.0
UK	28.5
USA	18.8
Sweden	29.6

Source: The Economist

Fig. 7.11 *Percentages employed in government services in selected countries, 1978*

Professional services

In all Japanese towns and cities there is a wide range of employment in professional services, such as architecture, law, advertising and dentistry, which are often linked with business services. In this section we can look at five examples of professional services.

1. *Education*

Although primary and high school teachers are classed as government employees, there are about a third of a million people teaching in private schools, colleges and universities (Fig. 7.10). Higher education is very much in demand in Japan, where one in every three students leaving senior high school goes on to study for a degree.

2. *Research*

Japan devotes much attention to research in all branches of science and technology. Some of this is carried out in universities (see Fig. 6.6), but much of it is not. Two-thirds of Japan's 282,000 researchers in 1980 were working for private companies and non-profit foundations. Among their main projects were space vehicles, advanced high speed trains, seabed exploration and miniature computers.

3. *Traditional culture*

More than any other industrial nation, Japan has held on to some of its medieval customs. Hence, thousands of Japanese work in traditional theatre, music and art, while an even greater number work full-time in more modern forms of culture, as artists, actors and musicians.

4. *Health and welfare*

Prior to World War II, large areas of Japan were poorly supplied with medical facilities. In recent years, however, hospitals and clinics have been provided throughout the country. By 1977, over three-quarters of a million people were working in this field.

5. *Communication*

Two branches of communication are important employers in the field of professional services. One is broadcasting. This includes commercial television and radio, together with NHK, which is a public corporation, rather like the BBC in Britain. In its 23-storey broadcasting centre in Tokyo, NHK has 6,000 employees, some looking after radio transmissions in over twenty different languages, while others operate the twenty-two TV studios, which work round the clock.

The other main branch of communication is journalism. The Japanese are such keen readers of newspapers that almost seventy million copies are sold daily, giving employment to many thousands of reporters and print workers.

In all five categories of professional service, there is a tendency for most of the

Fig. 7.12 *The Diet (parliament) building*

employment to be concentrated in the larger towns and cities.

Government services

Work for the national government and for local authorities makes up a smaller sector of employment in Japan than in any other advanced nation (Fig. 7.11). All the same, employees of the national government in 1980 numbered 1.2 million, the majority of them in the various ministries and agencies located in the Kasumigaseki district of central Tokyo (Fig. 7.12).

One reason for the relatively small number of government employees is that Japan, ever since the end of World War II, has very strictly limited the size of its armed forces. Where the United States, for instance, had over three million people in this category in 1980, Japan had only a quarter of a million. However, other Japanese government departments are large by any standards. For example, the Prime Minister's Office alone is responsible for several separate agencies, such as the Fair Trade Commission, the Imperial Household Agency and the Economic Planning Agency, which, in 1982, employed a total of 57,000 people.

Local government is also a major employer, with over 3.2 million public servants, including teachers, firemen, policemen, administrators and clerical workers. For local government purposes, Japan is divided into forty-seven prefectures, each containing cities, towns and villages which all have their own government officials.

One such is Kazuhira Nakamura, the mayor of Yachiyo. The city of Yachiyo, with a population of 130,000 in 1980, lies only thirty kilometres from Tokyo, and has grown quickly as a dormitory town for workers who commute daily to the capital. Yachiyo City provides civic centres and open spaces for its inhabitants, schools for their children and multi-storey housing blocks for those who prefer to rent rather than buy. Mayor Nakamura and his team of municipal administrators have to deal daily with requests and suggestions from Yachiyo residents, and the mayor also visits Tokyo frequently for negotiations with government officials. Overall, Nakamura's job is an important one, since his decisions can affect the daily lives of so many citizens.

Personal services

While central government services are a relatively small employer in Japan, personal services make up a larger sector. On the one hand, some of the older personal services (public baths attendant, seamstress, household servant) have been clearly declining. On the other hand, newer opportunities have been appearing, for example, in investigation agencies, telephone answering services and foreign language translation. While these changes go on, the main form of personal service is still, as it has been for centuries, entertainment.

Entertainment is a major employer for several reasons. One is that business firms in Japan set aside sizable sums of money with which to entertain clients. Jobs result, although many of them are low-status, poorly paid tasks, such as

Fig. 7.13 *Sumo wrestling*

washroom attendant, restaurant dishwasher or waitress. Yet, at the other end of the scale, Japan has some highly rewarded personal services. There are, for instance, many film studios, providing employment for lighting engineers, sound recordists and cameramen.

Again, like other advanced nations, Japan has professional sports organisations, especially in baseball and golf, although the percentage employed in full-time sport is lower than it would be in Europe of North America.

One example of professional sport, unique to Japan, is sumo wrestling. Sumo is an ancient sport which has become a modern favourite for television viewers. All sumo wrestlers are enormous men, weighing well over a hundred kilogrammes (Fig. 7.13). When opposing wrestlers clash, the result can be a spectacular battle, watched by millions.

In all modern cities, entertainment tends to occupy distinct areas in or near the centre. Japanese cities, as a rule, have large entertainment quarters, packed with hotels, bars, cafés, saunas, cabarets, cinemas and amusement arcades. Tokyo is large enough to have seven vast entertainment districts, where neon signs in an incredible mixture of shapes and colours light up the night-time crowds of pleasure-seekers.

Transport services

Japan's many urban centres are linked by various transport networks. Thus, there is a sector of service employment which involves airlines, railways, road haulage and passenger coach companies. In seaports, too, transport provides a wide range of jobs (Fig. 7.14). To illustrate this, we

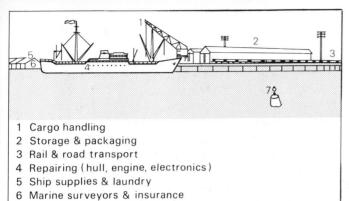

1 Cargo handling
2 Storage & packaging
3 Rail & road transport
4 Repairing (hull, engine, electronics)
5 Ship supplies & laundry
6 Marine surveyors & insurance
7 Pilotage, coastguard, tug services

Fig. 7.14 *Services linked to shipping*

can follow the activities surrounding just one of the twenty or so ships which enter or leave the port of Nagoya every day of the year.

On its regular run between Japan and Eastern Australia, the Norwegian cargo liner 'Martha Bakke' is today approaching Nagoya. At the entrance to Ise Bay, the ship passes Kamishima Island. From there, the signal station staff transmit a message to Nagoya Port Authority, giving the ship's estimated time of arrival.

Then, as the vessel approaches port, its name and other details are displayed on a computer-controlled screen which takes up a whole wall of one office in the Authority headquarters.

At the breakwater wall which shelters Nagoya harbour, the local pilot comes aboard to guide the ship on the last part of its journey. A harbour tug then helps the 'Martha Bakke' to berth at Inae Pier, where shore workers secure the vessel alongside. Other harbour employees then connect pipes to fill up the ship's supplies of fuel and fresh water. Immigration and customs officials make a thorough check of the ship's crew and their possessions. The following day, dockers will unload the 'Martha Bakke's' cargo of wool, semi-refined copper and tinned foods. Meanwhile, a harbour barge collects kitchen waste from the ship. The ship's agents, who handle all local business for the Knutsen Line, the owners of 'Martha Bakke', have arranged for a seaman to be driven to the port hospital to have an injured ankle X-rayed.

Fig. 7.15 *Part of Nagoya port*

To cope with the busy traffic of Nagoya port (Fig. 7.15), many more people are involved than those dealing with 'Martha Bakke'. Apart from several thousand dock workers, there are many truck drivers, who take cargoes to and from the docks, as well as maintenance employees, looking after the cargo-handling equipment, and hundreds of administrative employees in the offices of Nagoya Port Authority. If you remember that similar services have to be provided at all other major ports, such as Kobe, Yokohama and Osaka, and also at international air terminals, it is easy to understand that over five million people are employed in the entire national transport system.

Repair services

In a country which depends heavily on the constant use of machinery, it is important to have adequate repair services. Machines, after all, can break down at awkward moments. The demand for repair services is greatest in the major urban centres, where there are firms servicing electric lifts, office machinery and air conditioning, for example. At the other end of the urban scale, small towns with just a few thousand inhabitants would have repair facilities for cars, television sets and household electrical appliances. Overall, repair services are a much smaller employer than the other services mentioned in this chapter. At the same time, they are vital to the smooth working of the Japanese economy.

Central places

Services of different types are provided all over Japan in settlements of different sizes. These services are used not only by the inhabitants of the settlements but also by people from the surrounding rural area or *hinterland*. We use the term *central place* for any settlement which offers services. Depending on the services which they offer, central places can be arranged in a *hierarchy*, ranging from the largest city down to the smallest hamlet.

Central places at the upper end of the Japanese settlement hierarchy provide the highest order of service, used by great numbers of people over a very large area. Thus, small cities produce purely local newspapers, while medium-sized cities publish papers which serve entire regions. However, only Tokyo produces daily newspapers with an international circulation.

Central places at the upper level also have a larger number of establishments offering any given type of service. A small town of 4,000 people, for example, would probably have just one high school, whereas a huge city such as Tokyo would have hundreds of schools. Again, high level central places offer all those services found in lower level centres, while also offering services, such as television studios or foreign airline offices, which the lower level could never have.

Few countries have a national hierarchy of central places which has been established as long as that of Japan. As long ago as the eighth century, there was an urban system consisting of one major city, several main regional centres and many small district centres. Since then, this system has gradually developed into a vast and complicated arrangement of central places, as we will see in Chapter 11.

8 Living Standards

Introduction

Comparing the standards of living in various countries is far more difficult than you might at first think. Every human being has certain needs, such as food, clothing, housing and medical facilities. In addition to these, people have wants – extra things, which they could well do without but which they like to have. Examples include leisure facilities, private cars and all kinds of household gadgets. When we talk about high standards of living, then, we assume that all the basic needs are met, and that a large number of extras are also available.

There is no doubt that Japan has a high set of living standards, and this remains true, no matter how we try to measure these standards. Yet, there are some very real problems when we compare Japan with some of the other wealthy nations of the world. One important point is that Japanese culture, as we shall see later, is not quite like any other. Thus, Japanese people do not have exactly the same likes and dislikes as other nationalities. For example, wealthy Americans might well own a swimming pool, a home gymnasium and a small private aircraft. But for the Japanese, however rich they might be, it is simply not the custom to possess such things.

Again, we find that the richest countries, including the USA, Sweden and West Germany, all have a high daily consumption of meat (over 200 grammes per person, as Fig. 8.1 shows). Japan, by contrast, has a far lower consumption, but this fact does not make Japan a poor nation. It just means that in Japan, where space is very limited, farm animals have never been kept in large numbers. Hence, the traditional Japanese diet includes few animal products.

Modern life-styles

To see something of modern Japanese living standards, we can now look in detail at two particular individuals. No single person, of course, can properly represent a population of nearly 120 million. All the same, you do have to see how individuals live, so that you can put yourself in the place of the people of Japan.

1. *Toshio Matsuda*

Early morning commuting is extremely common in Japan. Toshio Matsuda, who is 50, is one of many workers who travel daily from the outer edge of Nagoya City to the Toyokawa locomotive works. Here, many different types of railway coach are built. Matsuda's job (Fig. 8.2) is to supervise a team of workers assembling the driver's cabin for trains running on Japan's super-express service – the Shinkansen. He has been working for the firm, Nippon Sharyo Seizo Company, since 1949. Now, as a senior employee, he

Fig. 8.1 *Meat intake in selected countries*

(grammes per person per day, 1977)

USA (1978)	320
Australia	294
W. Germany	248
Britain	201
Japan (1982)	89
China	61
Philippines	44

Source: Foreign Press Centre, Japan.

has a monthly wage of £630. Twice yearly, he also gets a bonus of over £1000.

Mr and Mrs Matsuda live with their two teenage daughters in a rather small four-roomed house, built of timber in the traditional Japanese style. Yet their house is crammed with electrical equipment, including a refrigerator, washing machine, toaster and colour television. The family eats well, using a mixture of western and Japanese meals. Each year, they take two short holidays; one to a company-sponsored hotel in the Japan Alps and another to tour northern or western Japan. At weekends, as a hobby, Matsuda often practises the ancient art of calligraphy (Fig. 8.3). Overall, his living standards are little different from those of any skilled worker in European industry.

2. Sachiko Hasegawa

The offices of large Japanese companies are staffed by a vast army of workers, most of them women. Tokyo, the main centre of office employment, is the home of many young women like Sachiko Hasegawa. Aged 25, she lives with her parents on the far north side of the great city, and travels by train each day to the headquarters of Suntory, a big distilling company. Since leaving college five years ago, Sachiko has worked in the finance department of her firm (see Fig. 8.4).

Her monthly salary is increased by special bonuses paid in July and December. Out of this, she pays about £40 into the family budget for food and accommodation. She saves about £60 per month for holidays, and has a personal fund which she can use some day when she marries and gives up work. The rest of her earnings is spent on fashion, eating out and on membership of a local tennis club. Sachiko enjoys a pleasant set of working surroundings by day, and a full social life with her friends when work is over.

Toshio Matsuda and Sachiko Hasegawa are just two people out of millions. There are some Japanese who live a good deal better than either, and likewise there are many others who are less affluent. Later

on, we shall see examples of this latter group.

Contrasts in life-styles

Different people follow different styles of living in Japan. For example, there are contrasts between townsfolk and farmers or between richer folk and poorer. However, one of the most obvious contrasts is

Fig. 8.2 *Toshio Matsuda at work on the 'bullet train'*

between modern and traditional ways of life.

Older people are more likely to live in the traditional types of Japanese house. These are built of wood and roofed with tile. The rooms are small, simple and rather bare, with sliding doors and heavy paper screens for walls (see Fig. 8.5). People sit on cushions on the living room floor, which is covered in straw matting (*tatami*). Bedding is stored in cupboards, to be laid out at night on the floor. In one room, the household would have a Buddhist memorial to the ancestors and also a god-shelf, containing various charms and souvenirs from some of Japan's great Shinto shrines.

The other rooms would probably include a cramped kitchen with little storage space, a room containing a deep, square bath-tub and a dry toilet which has to be pumped out regularly. The Japanese who live in this style of house would also follow other traditional ways of behaving. They might, for example, live as an extended family, with either an aged grandmother or a young married daughter sharing the home. Older members of the family would dress in either Japanese or western style, depending on the occasion. However, their western clothes would usually be rather old-fashioned. They would probably not own a car, not have travelled abroad and not be able to read any language other than Japanese.

When we look at the life-style of younger Japanese families, a quite different pattern appears. Thus, a typical family living within half an hour's travel of central Tokyo would have to occupy a small rented flat. One room might be fitted out in the traditional way, but the rest would have all kinds of up-to-date furnishings, bought from modern department stores. Traditional bedding, however, is still popular, and can be seen hanging out to air on the balconies of

Fig. 8.4 *Sachiko Hasegawa at work*

traditional houses and recently-built apartment blocks in every Japanese city.

The traditional bathroom is also still found throughout Japan where washing the body still takes place outside the bath, with the bath itself (which is much deeper than western baths) used only for warmth, refreshment and relaxation. The kitchen, on the other hand, would be much like those of any modern western home. Living in such a house might be a young married couple, with no children. Both would probably work full-time in the city, and their earnings would be enough to cover a local holiday in Japan every year (including skiing for example) and a foreign holiday occasionally. At weekends, they might visit bookshops, art galleries or concerts and eat out at some of Tokyo's countless restaurants. Their clothes would be fashionable and their conversation would include quite a few English words and phrases (see Fig. 8.6).

Here, we have been pointing out numerous details of traditional and modern life-styles in Japan. However, we must also stress that nowadays most Japanese are perfectly able to use both styles. Indeed, the ability to combine the old with the new is one of the outstanding features of Japanese life.

Fig. 8.3 *Calligraphy — widely practised in Japan and one of Toshio Matsuda's hobbies*

Fig. 8.5 *A traditional Japanese room*

Regional differences

An obvious fact of life in many countries is that one part of the nation may be very different from others. The Japanese, however, often argue that their own country is

Fig. 8.6 *English words borrowed into Japanese*

original	Japanese form
coffee	kohi
beer	biru
ice cream	aisukurimu
beefsteak	bifuteki
knife	naifu
ballpoint pen	borupen
handkerchief	hankachi
suit	sebiro
TV	terebi
orange	orenji
hotel	hoteru

an exception, because differences between the inhabitants of one region and those of another are hard to find. There are, of course, many variations in landscape and climate, but only slight differences in the way of life of the people. Throughout Japan, folk follow more or less the same customs, eat the same kinds of food and speak the same language (although not always easily understood because of strong regional dialects). Unlike so many other countries, Japan has no region in which a separate minority language is common, and no region where living standards are far below the national average.

Yet, some regional differences do exist. The richest Japanese live mainly in the great metropolitan centres of Tokyo, Nagoya and Kobe-Osaka-Kyoto. In other parts of the country, however, there are fewer highly paid jobs. These are the areas where houses are most likely to lack modern conveniences, where country roads may be poorly surfaced, and where some people have to travel long distances to shops and schools. The southern islands of Shikoku and Kyushu are examples, as are the northern district of Tohoku and the west coast area of Hokuriku; improvements in road systems and services in these areas, however, have been a feature of central government policy for some time.

Measuring standards of living

Whatever variations there may be between living standards in one part and another of Japan, it is between Japan and other countries that such differences can be most clearly seen. In this section, we can look at some ways of measuring the differences. In particular, we will pay attention to patterns of earning and spending money.

	US$
West Germany	9,356
Sweden	11,800
USA	11,694
France	9,362
Canada	10,277
Australia	9,518
Japan	7,740
U.K.	7,485
Greece	3,682
Korea (South)	1,469
Thailand	689

Source: 'International Financial Statistics'

Fig. 8.7 *National income per capita in selected countries*, 1982

Income

Most Japanese between the ages of 18 and 60 do some kind of paid work. Thus, if we examine the unemployment figures for a number of countries, we usually find that the Japanese are in a more fortunate position than most others. What is more, they are well rewarded for their work. It was once common to think of Japanese employees as being poorly paid, but this idea is completely out of date. Since the 1950s, the rate of growth for the whole Japanese economy has been higher than that of its competitors. Hence, Japanese firms can afford to pay their workers high wages. Indeed, at the very top of the scale, eight Japanese businessmen each had an annual income of over a million pounds in 1979. The most successful of all, Shokichi

Fig. 8.8 *Tax burdens in selected countries as a percentage of income*

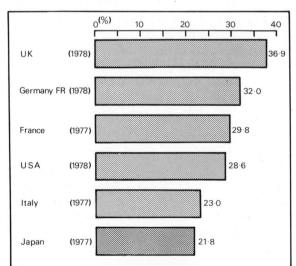

	(%)
UK (1978)	36.9
Germany FR (1978)	32.0
France (1977)	29.8
USA (1978)	28.6
Italy (1977)	23.0
Japan (1977)	21.8

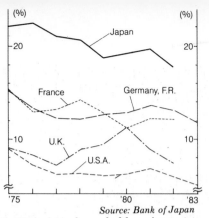

Fig. 8.9 Trends in household saving rates, 1975-83. (*Note: household saving rate = household saving ÷ household disposable income.*)

Source: Bank of Japan

Uehara, was earning no less than £11,000 per day.

One simple way of assessing a country's economic standing is to calculate its national income – that is the total value of all the work done by the country's residents in a year. If we divide the result by the number of residents in the country, we then have a statistic known as the national income per capita. Here again (Fig. 8.7), Japan ranks among the better off nations.

Before seeing how the Japanese spend their money, two points have to be mentioned.

1. High incomes can be reduced by deductions, such as income tax. In Japan, taxes are lower than in most other industrial nations (see Fig. 8.8), so the Japanese worker is left with a high proportion of his earnings, to spend as he wishes.

2. Earnings need not all be spent. The habit of saving is well established in Japan, and as Fig. 8.9 suggests the Japanese like to set money aside as a form of security. One reason for this has been that until recent years pensions and other forms of welfare payment were low in Japan.

Fig. 8.10 *Engel's coefficient for selected countries*

USA	20.1
Switzerland	21.6
Canada	26.8
Britain	28.2
Japan (1981)	27.5
Thailand	45.9

Source: Prime Minister's Office, Tokyo.

Country	Tap water supplies	Piped sewage facilities
Britain	99.4	98.0
W. Germany	99.3	87.7
Sweden	98.8	83.3
France	96.9	48.0
Japan	92.0	33.0

Souce: United Nations.

Fig. 8.11 *Percentage of households with basic amenities in selected countries, 1982*

Spending

The citizens of Japan spend their incomes in the following main ways.

1. *Food*

One way of judging standards of living is to measure how much of people's budgets is spent regularly on food. To measure this, the Engel's Coefficient, ranging up to a maximum of 100, is used. Richer nations eat well, but have a generally low coeffecient (below 40), because they have money left over to spend on housing, energy, clothes and entertainment. Fig. 8.10 shows Japan's high standing, comparable to that of Britain and Canada. Although the traditional Japanese diet of rice, vegetables and fish was well-balanced, in recent years people have been eating more meat, eggs and milk. As a result, the modern Japanese are as well nourished as their counterparts in any European nation.

2. *Housing*

In this case it is not so easy to show that the Japanese enjoy high standards. On the one hand, there are no homeless children roaming the streets, as there are in most other Asian countries. Makeshift shacks of waste timber and cardboard have long since disappeared from even the poorest quarters of Japanese cities. There is now a large stock of modern housing. Out of the total in 1980, 61 per cent was privately owned, while the rest was rented from private owners, from companies or from government agencies.

On the other hand, all is not well. One major complaint is that Japanese houses are too small by modern standards, and people therefore have difficulty fitting in all their belongings. Gardens are small or non-existent, and privacy is often hard to find in overcrowded urban areas. What is more, the basic household amenities of piped water and flush toilets are not as well provided (see Fig. 8.11) as in other advanced nations.

3. *Education*

To carry out all the jobs which have to be done in a modern economy, it is important to have an educated work force. Hence, educational spending is one of the main items in the budget of national and local government in Japan. Despite the enormous difficulty involved in learning to read and write Japanese, the nation has a good educational record. Few pupils leave school at the earliest possible date, and most actually go on to finish six years of secondary schooling. Equally well, a large proportion of young Japanese (Fig. 8.12) carry on to university, and the result is that industrial firms find it fairly easy to recruit graduates. Indeed, in many companies, 20 to 25 per cent of the labour force would have a university education. Companies can thus be confident that their

Fig. 8.12 *Proportion of young people going on to university, 1978*

USA	45.2
Japan	39.0
France	24.4
Britain	20.3

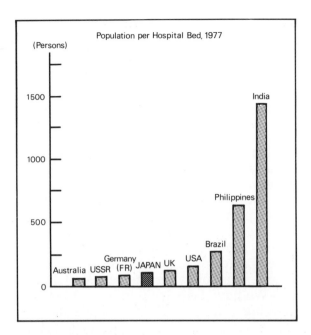

Fig. 8.13 *Persons per hospital bed in selected countries, 1977*

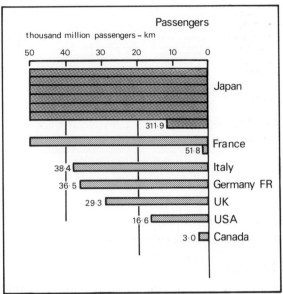

Fig. 8.14 *Rail passenger travel in selected countries, 1977*

employees understand the complex techniques and processes needed in modern industry.

4. *Health*

Here, too, Japan has a high international status. Like the other advanced countries, Japan has low numbers of population per doctor, or per hospital bed, as Fig. 8.13 shows. In addition, the long life expectancy of the average Japanese indicates high overall standards of public health. All the same, medical provision does vary from region to region, and people living near large cities have better facilities than those on the isolated offshore islands.

5. *Transport*

In all the advanced countries, there is constant movement of people and goods, and there are well developed networks for road, rail, air and sea transport. A common way of measuring transport activity is to calculate the number of travellers and the number of kilometres which they travel in a year. Fig. 8.14 illustrates this

statistic for rail travel in a number of countries, and the dominant position of Japan then becomes clear. A similar statistic for air travel would put Japan in second place internationally, but in road transport (measured in persons per vehicle) Japan's position would be slightly lower.

6. *Communications*

High living standards are also linked to the levels of communication within a country. In the case of Japan, we can measure communications in a variety of

Fig. 8.15 *Telephones per 100 persons in selected countries, 1977*

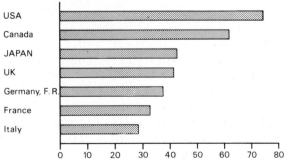

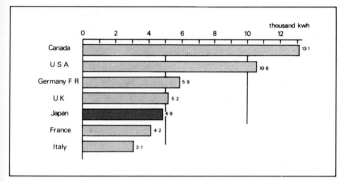

Fig. 8.16 *Use of electricity per capita in selected countries, 1978*

ways: the number of television receivers per thousand persons, the number of telephones per thousand persons, or the number of newspapers bought daily. Fig. 8.15 shows that Japan again ranks high on the international scale. In the same way, Japan is the only Asian country with nationwide television and an enormous daily circulation of newspapers. One paper, the *Yomiuri Shimbun*, was selling nearly 13.5 million daily copies (combined circulation of morning and evening papers) in 1983.

7. *Energy*

A large demand for various forms of energy is a very useful indicator of high standards of living. Japan demonstrates this by importing more coal and oil than any other nation for its industries. Likewise, Japanese homes are generally well served with supplies of gas and electricity. An international comparison (Fig. 8.16) illustrates the heavy use of electricity in Japan. Although the example only shows two nations below Japan, many other countries are in a similar position. Meanwhile, some of the countries above Japan have a high placing because they use electricity rather wastefully in domestic heating.

8. *Crime*

High living standards are of little value if they cannot be enjoyed in peace and security. Thus, some advanced countries (such as the USA) and some less developed

Crimes recorded per 100,000 people, 1981.

USA	5519
Britain	4137
Japan	1085

Source: National Police Agency, Japan

Fig. 8.17 *Crime rates in selected countries, 1978*

nations (like Jamaica or Colombia) have serious problems of crime. In Japan, however, offences such as robbery, assault and murder are less common than in most other parts of the world. Even the overcrowded cities are usually safe places, and when crimes are committed (Fig. 8.17) the rate of arrest is high. This, we could argue, is an extra bonus for the people of Japan.

We have been looking here at ways of judging Japanese living standards. Another way of assessing a country's state of advancement is to look at the social welfare provided for its citizens.

Social welfare

In the past, Japan had nothing like the social welfare system found in European countries since the beginning of this century. Three main reasons for the lack of public welfare in Japan were:

i) People were expected to do for themselves many of the things which we in Britain have expected the government to provide. Families looked after their own elderly relatives, for example, instead of sending them to an old folks' home. Equally, the idea of abandoning children, to have them taken into official care, was almost unknown.

ii) For some people at least, employers provided the benefits which British workers would get from the government. This is still the case, and company pensions in Japan are often preferred to State pensions.

iii) The proportion of aged, dependent people in Japan was low, and it is only in very recent years that it has begun to grow considerably. Elderly people of course, do put extra demands on the welfare system.

These three reasons are not as strong today as they once were, and Japan has now followed the other industrial nations by offering its citizens a wide range of social services. We can judge this by the fact that in 1963 the value of these benefits came to only five per cent of the national income, but by 1980 the figure had gone up to fifteen per cent. Public funds for welfare are paid out in three main ways.

1. *Medical insurance and public health*

Everyone who is employed in Japan pays a regular sum for medical insurance, and is therefore entitled when ill to get medical treatment and cash benefits. The cost is borne partly by employers and partly by the national and local governments, who also pay for hospitals, health centres and ambulance services. In the same way, people who are not covered by medical insurance are still able to get help from public funds.

2. *Pensions*

In Japan, a state pension is paid to everyone who is over the official retirement age of 60. Under the state scheme, pensions in theory can represent as much as 44 per cent of earnings in the year immediately before retirement — a proportion which is quite high in comparison with pension payments in western countries. In practice, however, pension payments vary according to the length of time over which the recipient has been insured under the scheme. Since the scheme was introduced only in 1961, few people as yet qualify for full pensions, and the government's total expenditure on pension payments remains low by western standards.

This situation will change drastically in the years ahead, as more and more people qualify for full pension payments. It is estimated, for example, that the proportion of the population aged 65 and over, which stood at 9.6 per cent in 1982, will rise to 15.6 per cent by the year 2000. Thus, pension and welfare payments for the elderly are bound to represent a growing burden on state expenditure.

3. *Other public welfare services*

Assistance is also given, for instance, to those who are out of work. Compared to Britain, however, Japan has far fewer people who would qualify for this kind of benefit. In addition, the government helps to provide for those unfortunate people who are physically or mentally handicapped. Throughout the country, special centres have also been set up for the care of the aged.

Japan, then, has been developing its welfare systems beyond what other Asian countries can offer. Yet, other problems remain. Social overhead capital, also known as the infrastructure, includes such public facilities as parks, schools, drainage schemes, roads and housing. Japan has partly neglected these, by putting so much of its resources into industrial capital, such as factory buildings and equipment. As a result, her manufacturing output is among the world's largest, but the infrastructure has lagged far behind.

Similarly, public housing is not easy to find, for those who cannot afford to buy their own houses. Indeed, only about seven per cent of all houses in Japan were being rented by government agencies in 1980. Thus, despite the welfare provisions being made in Japan, there is further scope for improvement.

Japan's minority groups

Centuries ago, the Japanese population was arranged into four main classes. Some people, however, fell below even the bottom group, because they carried out work which was thought to be unclean. Such jobs included animal slaughtering, leather working and well digging. By the 1600s, people in these outcaste groups were being made to show their low status by wearing distinctive clothing and by living apart from other Japanese. During the last hundred years, Japanese of outcaste origin have been referred to as 'burakumin', or 'people from special communities'.

Other 'outside' groups include people of Korean origin who numbered some 674,000 in 1983. Korea was a colony under Japanese rule from 1910 to 1945, and during that time many thousands of Koreans were brought to Japan to find employment as labourers and factory workers. Thus, the Korean-born population grew from 40,000 in 1920 to over 400,000 in 1930. Today, their descendants are denied full Japanese citizenship, and are classed instead as 'permanent residents'.

By contrast, the Ainu people can claim to have been in northern Japan before the modern Japanese ever occupied that area. The Ainu not only have a different appearance from the Japanese but also have a quite different set of beliefs and customs. Thus, though there has been much inter-marriage between the groups, and although Japanese is now spoken by all, the Ainu remain a distinct minority. They have all the rights of other Japanese citizens, and yet are treated as a quaint, old-fashioned group, very much like the Indians in North America.

On the one hand, tourists flock through Ainu villages (Fig. 8.18), buying native crafts and photographing traditional customs. On the other hand, unemployment in these villages is above average and the living conditions of many elderly Ainu are extremely poor. One-roomed dwellings in a low state of repair are common. Yet another problem is the divided opinion between those Ainu who make a profit from tourism and those others who say it is degrading to sell one's heritage to casual visitors. Meanwhile, of the 15,000 Ainu who remain in the northern island of Hokkaido, only a few hundred could claim to be of pure descent.

Rather like the Ainu in the north, the Okinawans in the south also happened to live in an area which became part of Japanese territory. Though little different in appearance from other Japanese, the Okinawans have had a different history and speak a dialect of their own.

*   *   *

One other group on the fringe of society is made up of the thousands of foreigners, including businessmen, writers and professors, who are resident in Japan. No matter how well they learn to speak and write in Japanese, they will always remain outsiders, or 'gaijin'. However, they do at least have the compensation of a fairly high standard of living. The same is not true of many Japanese of inter-racial parentage. During the years of American occupation (1945–52), a number of children were born of Japanese mothers and coloured American fathers. Their appearance has made it difficult for them to be accepted by the rest of the Japanese population, and as a group they tend to have poor job prospects.

Fig. 8.18 *A winter ritual in an Ainu village*

Japanese culture

Every large grouping of human beings has its own collection of ideas and habits, passed on from one generation to the next. These ways of thinking and behaving are usually the ones which have best helped members of the group to deal with their surroundings. The word 'culture' is often used to describe all that people inherit from the society into which they are born. Although we cannot examine Japanese culture in detail here, we can at least look at three of its main features.

1. *Culture on the surface*

One of the most obvious ways in which a culture shows itself is in its language, and certainly no other language is quite like Japanese. Wherever you travel in Japan, you find countless printed signs. These may seem very confusing, but a close look tells you that there are actually three scripts, which can all be used together in any one sentence (see Fig. 8.19). One script (*katakana*) is for foreign words borrowed into Japanese, another (*hiragana*) is for simple Japanese words, while the third (*kanji*) is used for more complicated words and is comprised entirely of Chinese characters. Altogether, there are several thousand characters; however, school children are required to learn approximately 1930 kanji, plus the katakana and hiragana 'alphabets' that have 46 'letters' each. So, you can imagine what a difficult task learning Japanese is.

Another outward sign of Japan's distinct culture is in types of dress. Though most Japanese now wear western clothes, the older ways can still be seen (Fig. 8.20). For women, traditional dress includes an outer gown (*kimono*), a heavy waist sash (*obi*) and thonged, flat footwear (*zori*) (see Fig. 8.22). For men, there is the house gown (*yukata*) worn at home for relaxation at the end of the working day. There is also the headband (*hachimaki*) which is worn as a sign of determined effort by labourers at work, students at examinations and protesters on the march.

Japanese culture also shows itself in the various pastimes which are part of the country's traditions. Flower arrangement (*ikebana*) is one example, based on rules dating back over several centuries. *Bonsai*, the art of growing miniature trees in shallow pots, and paper-folding (*origami*) have also been borrowed from

Fig. 8.19 *An introduction to Japanese writing*

Examples of the three Japanese scripts

Katakana

スコットランド
= sukottorando
= Scotland

クリスマス
= kurisumasu
= Christmas

Hiragana

はちまき
= hachimaki
= headband

きもの
= kimono
= robe or gown

Kanji

書
= sho
= calligraphy

団体
= dantai
= group

Fig. 8.20 *Traditional and contemporary dress amongst members of a Japanese farming family*

Japan by the nations of the West. On a more aggressive note, Japanese culture has also developed such sports as *kendo*, *sumo* wrestling, *karate* and *aikido*.

2. *Faiths and festivals*

It is unusual for a country to combine two very different religions, without obvious stress. In Japan, however, the two national faiths are Shinto, which is entirely Japanese; and Buddhism, which was taken from India, via China and Korea, at least fourteen hundred years ago. Far from being in conflict, these two religions have got on well with each other. It is still customary for Japanese to go through Shinto ceremonies in infancy and at marriage, while funeral proceedings are conducted on Buddhist lines. One or two Buddhist teachings are widely heeded. Thus, an important lesson is that life in this world is very temporary, and that things of beauty quickly pass. Even in the first year of primary school, this idea is put over to children by poems like the one which says:

'*Though the blossom be fragrant*

The flower will fall
Who in this world of ours
Will last forever?'

Shinto shrines and Buddhist temples dot the landscape of Japan, and each faith has its own annual festivals at various places. The religious side of Japanese festivals is now less important than the public processions, where vast crowds gather to watch decorated floats being pulled through the streets, to the constant accompaniment of drums, bells and flutes. Other festivals, however, take place in the home. On 3 March, for example, schoolgirls celebrate 'Girls' Day' (Fig. 8.21) by dressing up, inviting friends in to eat special dishes and to view each other's doll collections.

3. *Social rules*

The Japanese think that social rules are extremely important, and some of these rules make life in Japan quite different from what it is in other lands. We have room here to mention just two examples.

i) *Politeness.* It is the everyday behaviour of the Japanese people which makes their country unlike all others.

Fig. 8.21 *'Girls Day' festival on 3 March*

Fig. 8.22 *The Japanese form of greeting*

Behaving correctly is a very basic rule. In a crowded land, politeness helps to make life a little easier. Thus, people bow on meeting (Fig. 8.22) and they also use different words for different levels of politeness. For instance, the word for 'I' is *'boku'* if one is talking to friends, but *'watakushi'* when one is speaking to someone demanding greater respect.

    ii) *Agreement.* In Japanese society, people generally try to find agreement or consensus. Whatever the problem, it can always be discussed by everybody concerned, until eventually some sort of joint solution is found. In industry, this way of working has at least one great advantage. It makes employees feel that they are in touch with what is going on and that their opinion is of some value. Hence, they are not likely to take sudden strike action.

Values

Whatever society in the world you happen to study, you will find that there is some

Fig. 8.23 *School uniform*

set of values, with which most people in the society agree. These values and beliefs always show up clearly in the life of the country. In Britain, for example, where patience and orderliness are two traditional values, it is not surprising that queues are a regular sight. So, too, in Islamic countries, where religious values still hold, it is common to see women modestly veiled and to hear loudspeakers calling the faithful to prayer. Japan has its own values, which play a part in the geography of the nation, and here we can look at three of these.

1. *Hard work*

When Japanese society was rural and agricultural, farming families had to get used to long periods of very hard work. The harsh Japanese winter meant that a surplus of food had to be gathered during the other months of the year. Similarly, in

the many coastal fishing villages, people had to endure long hours of toil, often in bitter cold and damp, to make a living. In the traditional craft industries, like textiles, pottery and paper-making, the same need for concentrated effort was always present. None of this has been forgotten in Japan, although the jobs in question have themselves changed. The continuing belief in hard work is perhaps encouraged by the fact that most people work in groups, and group activity is itself a source of pleasure.

2. *Group loyalty*

The most basic group in Japan, as in the West generally, is the family unit, Yet, though the Japanese live their own private lives much as we do, they also spend more of their time in groups. Work groups are especially common, and many Japanese would argue that they gain a lot from group membership, whether in a giant industrial company or in a small local firm. Employers are expected to act like the heads of families, and one result is that people working for the same firm are more aware of their shared membership than of any differences between managers and other workers. The family and the firm, of course, are just two examples of groups. In days gone by, it was even common to think of all Japan as one great national group, with the Emperor as its family head.

3. *Discipline*

Everybody in Japan is expected to know and obey the rules of their society and to keep their own private wishes firmly in control. This kind of discipline shows itself in many ways. It means, for example, that children always wear uniform to high school (Fig. 8.23), that public transport runs exactly to its timetable and that vandalism is almost unknown. Again, it means that workers pay careful attention to what they are doing. Thus, Japanese television sets are assembled more quickly and with fewer faults on average than European sets. At work, too, discipline means that latecoming and walk-outs are very unusual. Discipline, then, goes along with hard work and also with suffering in silence. One drawback is that these same qualities which have favoured Japanese industry have made the Japanese people put up with rather a lot, by way of desperately crowded transport and dangerously polluted air.

9 Conservation And Recreation

Conservation

Wherever there are mines and factories, pollution problems appear in the surrounding air, water and living systems. In Japan, the natural environment has been damaged in countless ways, ever since modern industry began to grow during the 1870s. Although anti-pollution measures were started at a fairly early date in Japan, they were ignored more and more as manufacturing expanded. Thus, during the period 1920–70, industrial pollution became extremely widespread in Japan, which was referred to worldwide as a nation on the verge of poisoning itself.

One writer described Japan as 'an octopus eating its own legs'. The word *kogai*, meaning 'public nuisance', began to appear daily in press and television reports. Over the past decade or so, many improvements have at last taken place, although much pollution remains. Pedestrians can still taste the traffic fumes in central Tokyo, for example, and river pollution is far from being solved. Yet, in this section, we shall see how the Japanese have tried hard to set better standards for the conservation of their injured natural environment.

Air pollution

Waste gases, such as sulphur dioxide or carbon monoxide, together with dust particles are scattered into the air from factory chimneys, vehicle exhausts and mining operations. Here is what resulted in the case of two Japanese cities.

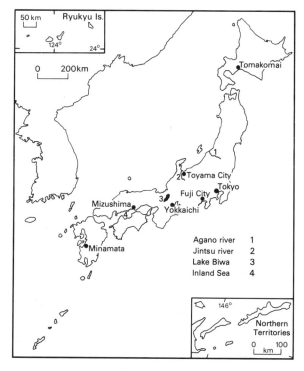

Fig. 9.1 *Locations mentioned in the text*

1. *Yokkaichi* (see Fig. 9.1) lies on the sheltered west side of Ise Bay. During 1955, Japan's biggest oil refinery and petro-chemicals complex was set up here, on land where the Imperial Japanese Navy once had a vast fuel depot. Over the following eight years, other new chemical plants spread across the coastal flats, on which farmers' crops had previously ripened in the summer sun. As a result, the industrial output of this area grew three times as fast as the national average between 1955 and 1970.

Yet the companies which were growing rich from the new industries around Yokkaichi were also causing serious difficulties for local inhabitants. From

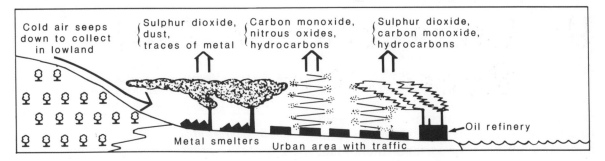

Fig. 9.2 *Sources of air pollution*

1959 onwards, so many people began to complain of constant coughing, chest pains and breathing problems that the name 'Yokkaichi asthma' came into use Eventually, a group of the sufferers brought a court case against six of the petroleum, chemicals and electricity companies which had polluted the surrounding air. It took several years for the court to reach a decision, but in the end the offending companies were ordered to pay the complainants a sum equivalent to £150,000.

2. *Tokyo* has long had one of the world's greatest concentrations of vehicle traffic. On windless days, hundreds of thousands of car exhausts fill the city air with a faint blue haze of carbon monoxide, nitrogen oxides, lead and hydrocarbons (unburnt petrol). As the sun shines down on this gassy mixture, photochemical smog is formed. One day in June 1970, girls at Rissho High School, who had been taking physical education in the school playground, were affected by sore throats, running eyes, breathing difficulties and numb limbs.

At the time air pollution was nine times greater than the daily average for Tokyo, and it is hard to believe that there was no connection between the pupils' condition and the chemical poisons in the air they were breathing. In this case, however, the blame could not easily be attached to any particular culprit. All the same, as we shall see, action has been taken to at least reduce the occurrence of this type of air pollution.

Yokkaichi and Tokyo are by no means unusual in Japan, where certain sources (Fig. 9.2) constantly produce wastes which affect the quality of the air. Since factories and vehicles have been the main sources, it is on these that we will focus.

1. *Factories*

Along the eastern sea-board of Japan, fringed by one industrial town after another, there is something strange about the air. On most days, you cannot see very far and the sunlight filters weakly through a yellow mist — the same atmospheric mixture which caused Yokkaichi asthma. Most common among the waste gases in the air is sulphur dioxide, which damages human lungs as well as vegetation and buildings. However, the Japanese have now managed to reduce the amounts of waste sulphur dioxide, by using the following measures:

i) By reducing the quantity of heavy petroleum, rich in sulphur, imported daily from the Arabian Gulf. This can only be achieved if other forms of fuel, such as nuclear and natural gas, are used instead.

ii) By spending money on special equipment for removing the sulphur from imported petroleum, and for desulphurising the waste gases given off by power stations, steel mills and oil refineries.

iii) By building very tall chimneys, which help to keep the unwanted gases away from the ground. Unfortunately, many Japanese towns lie on low land, surrounded by hills which prevent the easy escape of polluted air.

2. Vehicles

Out of vehicle exhausts there comes, as we have seen, a dangerous mixture of polluting materials. As long ago as 1972, the Japanese government decided to set emission standards for new cars. Eventually, no car travelling on Japanese roads would be allowed to give off more than a certain minimum amount of carbon monoxide, nitrogen oxides or hydrocarbons. These standards have been made ever more strict, and, although Japanese car makers have been able to meet them, very few foreign-built cars are designed to cope. As a result, the air in Japanese city centres was rather clearer in 1980 than it had been in 1970.

Air pollution from factories and vehicles is also covered by the Air Pollution Control Act, passed in 1968. As in the United States, the national government sets the main guidelines, but local governments are free to impose even stricter standards, if they so wish. For this purpose, a network of air monitoring stations, right across the country, allows Japanese officials to check on the pollution being produced at any given time.

Water pollution

Japan is by nature a country of clear upland streams, and shorelines rich in marine life. Fresh water is needed to fill Japanese rice-fields, fish-ponds and wash-basins. But, during the past hundred years, the Japanese have been busy poisoning their own vital supplies of water.

Fig. 9.3 shows just a sample of the ways in which the damage has been done. From intensively farmed fields, fertilisers and pesticides are washed out into rivers and lakes. From millions of homes, domestic sewage is poured out seawards, while Japan's factories have been allowed over the years to quietly empty some of

1 Waste hot water, reducing oxygen capacity of water.
2 Dust & fibres coat water surface, inhibiting life.
3 Dissolved fertiliser causing plant growth.
4 Surface effluents (e.g. oil, detergents) inhibiting marine l
5 Chemical poisons (acids, alkalis, metals).
6 Sewage, using up oxygen in water.

Fig. 9.3 *Sources of water pollution*

the most dangerous of poisons into nearby drainage systems. To show the effects of water pollution on ordinary people in Japan, we can look in detail at three cases.

1. The small industrial town of *Minamata* (Fig. 9.1) in western Kyushu was dominated for many years by one large chemicals factory. In the 1940s, the firm began to use mercury in the making of vinyl material, and the poisonous wastes from this process were discharged into the nearby bay. Then, from 1953 onwards, a strange sequence of events took place. Dead fish floated in the shallows, seabirds made fatal crash landings and pet cats danced around wildly before dropping dead. Local people complained of deafness, tremors and overall weakness. Soon, newborn children in Minamata were showing severe defects, including blindness, twisted limbs and severe mental handicap.

Behind all this lay one important fact. Fish from the polluted waters of Minamata Bay were a major item in the diet of the sufferers, human and animal alike. In the end, a long and bitter lawsuit was brought against the company in 1969, and four years later damages totalling £1.2 million were awarded to the victims. By then, however, over a hundred had died and the lives of hundreds more had been permanently ruined. Meanwhile, a very similar case had occurred on the Agano River, in northwest Japan, and here, too, compensation was eventually paid to the victims.

2. Mining for metals such as copper and zinc produces large quantities of rock waste, usually containing traces of other metals, like lead or cadmium. Cadmium,

Fig. 9.5 *The natural beauty of Lake Biwa*

Fig. 9.4 *Lake Biwa and its surroundings*

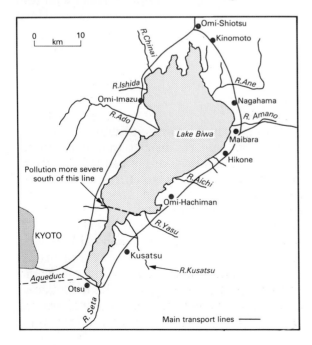

when it gets into the human system, has the power to eat away at the calcium which makes up bones. The victim in such cases suffers agonising pain, as his spine crumbles within, leaving him a helpless cripple. During the 1960s, at least seven different areas in Japan were producing this form of pollution, and among them was *Toyama City*, on the Jinzu River (Fig. 9.1). Upstream from the town, cadmium-tainted drainage from the Kamioka mine and smelter had poisoned the irrigation water used for local rice production. Here, again, the victims finally had to sue the offending company, which denied any liability but had in the end to pay up.

3. The largest freshwater body in Japan is *Lake Biwa* (Figs. 9.4, 9.5). Since 1960, there has been increasing pressure on the

southern end of this lake, where the food, machinery and electronics industries have been growing. As a result, fish catches in the area have been contaminated by chemical effluents. At the same time, while population in the surrounding area of Shiga Prefecture climbed towards the one million level, the sewage wastes from this population were finding their way into the lake. Human wastes, plus excess fertilisers draining from neighbouring farmlands, cause heavy weed growth around the lake shores.

This change, which is known as eutrophication, can have very undesirable results. Every lake has, dissolved in its water, a quantity of oxygen, which tends to give the lake a naturally clear, sparkling appearance. However, any waste material which decays in the lake water puts a demand (known as the biological oxygen demand, or BOD) on the dissolved oxygen. A high BOD, such as exists at the southern end of Lake Biwa, uses up oxygen and leaves the water dull, lifeless and hardly suitable for human consumption. Yet, this same water has to provide drinking supplies for the cities of Kyoto, Osaka and Kobe.

The problems of water pollution in Japan have been so severe that some kind of legislation had eventually to be introduced. The government's first major step was to pass, in 1967, the Basic Law for Environmental Pollution Control. In 1971, the Environment Agency was set up as the national body concerned with laws on pollution. Yet, not everybody agrees about the usefulness of such laws. The Japanese Association of Manufacturers, for instance, views them as being hard on industry, while others (including journalists, scientists and relatives of victims) criticise the rules for being too easy-going.

In all, the control of air pollution has been more successful than that of water pollution although schemes to improve water quality in the bays of Tokyo, Ise and Osaka have been successful. The discharge of the most dangerous liquid chemicals is now strongly discouraged, yet there is far less supervision over other effluents, such as pulp waste. Thus, citizens of *Fuji City*, a large paper-making centre in Shizuoka Prefecture, felt compelled in 1977 to sue their local government for allowing nearby Tagonoura Port to become almost clogged by pollution from four paper mills. At the same time, there are other more encouraging signs, such as the revival of angling since 1980 in the waters around Tokyo Bay.

Pollution by solids

Japan in the past was a nation with no serious problem of solid waste disposal. Peasant households fed their scraps to hens and pigs, while townsfolk were not yet rich enough to produce many leftovers. Sewage was still used as a fertiliser for crops. But there have been quite remarkable changes since the 1950s. As Japanese industries have expanded, they have produced vast quantities of solid waste. Meanwhile, as the Japanese people have grown richer, so they have been able to discard items (including refrigerators, washing machines and furniture) which in previous times they could not even afford to own.

The problem of solid waste is dealt with in four main ways.

i) *Incineration*

Although the burning of household refuse can itself lead to further pollution of the air, most Japanese cities use this method, simply because it is so convenient.

ii) *Recycling*

In recent years, there has been a strong trend towards new use of waste materials, such as paper and glass. Indeed, some Japanese manufacturers, like Sumitomo Cement, have begun to use fuel oil derived from discarded tyres.

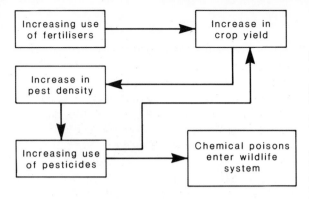

Fig. 9.6 *Effects of using pesticides*

iii) *Infill*

Japan carries out more land reclamation than any other country. Around Tokyo Bay, for example, solid blocks of dry compressed garbage have been used over the years to create extensive areas of new land These are now used for industry, housing projects and for recreation.

iv) *Ocean dumping*

Another less satisfactory method is to carry barge-loads of urban refuse out for dumping in the inshore waters of the Pacific Ocean.

Ecological damage

Living things in the natural environment can be very seriously affected by human activities. On land, the forests which cover most of Japan have been shrinking, partly because their timber is wanted by the paper manufacturers and partly because air pollution has been gradually damaging them. So, too, as their habitat becomes more limited, birds and other wildlife are harder to find. Although hundreds of

refuges have been set up, within which wildlife is protected, licensed hunting still goes on in the uplands of Japan. Down in the agricultural lowlands, the heavy use of pesticides also discourages wildlife.

Japanese farmers spray large amounts of chemicals on to their cultivated fields, but this in turn causes new problems, as Fig. 9.6 suggests. While several of these chemicals have been officially banned in Japan, it takes years for them to disappear from natural systems. For some living species, therefore, the passing of the National Environment Preservation Law (1973) may have come rather too late.

In the waters of Japan, living things have also suffered severely. Sometimes, the ecological damage is quite intentional. Thus, the Tomakomai Fishermen's Co-operative in Hokkaido accepted compensation worth £10 million in 1975, when a vast new industrial port was developed on their fishing grounds. On the other hand, the harm may be quite accidental. In 1974, a damaged tank leaked an enormous oil spill into the Inland Sea at Mizushima, and the company responsible had to pay local fishermen for the damage done to marine life.

Despite the laws which have been passed to limit pollution, the Inland Sea remains a problem area. The reclamation of new land along the shoreline continues to reduce the area where fish can be farmed and edible seaweed grown. Poisonous chemical wastes still find their way into the water, and then build up in natural food chains (Fig. 9.7).

Another difficulty, all through the 1970s, has been the so-called 'red tides' of

Fig. 9.7 *How poisonous chemicals build up in natural food chains*

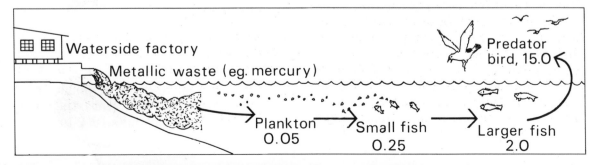

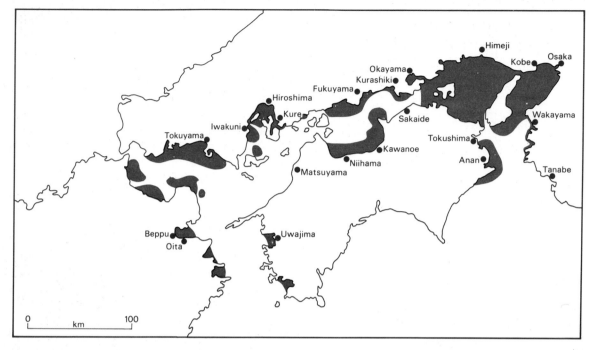

Fig. 9.8 *Distribution of red tides in the Inland Sea (1972)*

the Inland Sea (Fig. 9.8). Chemical waste, such as phosphorous, encourages the growth of certain microscopic marine creatures, which can then poison millions of valuable fish. Because this sea is almost completely cut off from the open Pacific, it takes a long time for its refuse to be washed away. Meanwhile, even the passing of the Seto Inland Sea Conservation Law in 1973 has not been enough to stop the destruction of living systems in the area.

Noise pollution

In Japan, the problem of noise pollution has been especially severe, because traditional houses have very little insulation against noise, while noisy factories are usually situated among houses. Until recently, there was hardly any opposition to this and other forms of pollution, since the Japanese custom was to patiently endure discomfort. However, changes have been appearing. For instance, there

are now government standards for permitted noise levels, applying to factories and vehicles. There are also signs that ordinary people can take action against noise pollution.

Local opposition has delayed the building of a main highway in the port of Yokohama, and the construction of a high-speed railway line north of Tokyo. Where expressways cut through housing zones, as at Kita Karasuyama in Tokyo, canopies have been built over the road, to reduce the effects of traffic noise. But other noise problems are more difficult to solve. Busy airports, like Osaka and Tokyo's Haneda airport, where aircraft land or take off on average every few minutes, happen to lie very close to extensive areas of housing. Likewise, the shortage of space in Japanese cities condemns thousands of urban dwellers to live within a few metres of railway lines (Fig. 9.9) and ring roads.

Overview

It is now obvious that the people of Japan are no longer as tolerant of pollution as they once were. In recent years, they have adopted the idea known as PPP (polluter-

Fig. 9.9 *Elevated railway in built-up area*

pays principle), which means that companies convicted of causing dangerous pollution are likely to have to pay compensation. They are also liable to fines, although rich industrial corporations are not much troubled by trifling fines, it must be admitted.

Recreation

Conservation is needed, to protect the Japanese environment from the worst effects of pollution. The environment has to be guarded for its own sake, and also because it is so important for recreation. Recreation, in turn, plays a vital part in the Japanese economy, since it provides a wide range of employment and produces mass movements of people throughout the country.

Over the past twenty years, all kinds of leisure facilities have been increasing in Japan. For one thing, the average citizen is now richer and is therefore in a better position to spend money on pastimes. What is more, retired people and students, two of the groups most likely to have time for recreation, have grown steadily in number. Yet, this stress on enjoyment may come as a surprise to anyone who had thought of the Japanese simply as very hard-working folk.

However, we do have to notice that patterns of recreation in Japan are not always the same as those found in Britain and other western countries. One difference is that the Japanese are generally keen on group outings. Hence, any leisure facility, whether it be a skating pond in winter or a lake shore in summer, is likely to be packed with families, school parties

Fig. 9.11 *Lake Hakone*

and other groups. Another difference is that the Japanese tend to get shorter holidays than workers in western countries, and they may not even take all the leave to which they are entitled. As a result, short breaks of three of five days are extremely common, and these would often be spent touring inside Japan.

A third difference is that the Japanese are far more likely to use their leisure in a way connected with their work. Firms hold regular excursions and sports days, for example, while fellow employees often meet in social groups when work is finished. There are other differences, as we shall see. Meanwhile, we can arrange recreation into five categories, each of which makes its own impact on the environment.

Local amenities

Most Japanese are town dwellers, and it is

Fig. 9.10(a) *Baseball — Japan's leading spectator sport;* **(b)** *one of Japan's many golf ranges*

in towns that they carry out many of their leisure activities. Local recreation in Japan takes place mainly outside the home, and so every town has a distinct pleasure area, quite different from anything you might find in a middle-sized British town. After normal working hours, Japanese urban centres seem to be almost as busy as during the day. Traffic is heavy. The pavements are crowded with people, while overhead the countless flashing neon signs indicate nightclubs, bars, amusement arcades and theatres. In fact, in any of the larger cities there would be thousands of leisure establishments, forming entire night-life districts. One factor which has encouraged the growth of these areas is the Japanese tax system, which has allowed firms to spend freely on entertainment as a business expense.

On the other hand, Japanese towns are generally poorly provided with parks and playgrounds. Beyond the town, there are few places where one can stroll, because intensive farming is so common. Again, although many towns are near the coast, few have public beaches. People from Tokyo, for example, use the Shonan beaches, about an hour's journey to the south of the city. However, up to a million visitors might come here on a summer weekend, and the overcrowding which results is quite beyond anything ever found in Britain.

Yet the average Japanese town does at least offer a variety of modern facilities for recreation, such as tennis courts, baseball grounds (Fig. 9.10(a)) and swimming pools. Golf is a popular game, but there is little space for proper golf courses, so players usually have to make do with golf driving ranges (Fig. 9.10(b)). These large net-protected enclosures are a common sight throughout Japan. Leisure facilities like these are user-oriented. That is to say they are created close to where potential customers live. By contrast, resource-oriented facilities such as beautiful landscapes and hot springs may be found a long way from the main centres of population.

Scenic areas

Resource-oriented leisure facilities are often based on some sort of natural feature, like the example in Fig. 9.11. Japan is a land of mountains, some of which are active or extinct volcanoes. By tradition, volcanoes were viewed with awe, since they showed the violent and unpredictable forces of nature. Mount Fuji, the highest peak in Japan, received special attention. Its vast cone shape makes it the ideal mountain, and it is used on postage stamps and wall posters as a national symbol.

In Japanese art, views of the snow-topped mountain from a long distance are common. Indeed, in other parts of the country, volcanic peaks (like Yoteisan in Hokkaido or Iwakisan in northern Honshu) which resemble Mount Fuji are also particularly admired. From the tourist's point of view, volcanic uplands have an

Fig. 9.13 *Areas of outstanding beauty (Japan's National Parks)*

extra advantage, in the form of hot springs (Fig. 9.12). These tie in with the Shinto stress on cleanliness, and in suitable areas communal bath houses were often set up in the past. Nowadays, modern motels and spas have grown around some of these spots and are highly popular tourist attractions.

Mountains in general are an important leisure resource in Japan. Quite apart from visitors who are drawn by the scenery, crowds of climbers and winter ski enthusiasts are also attracted. Yet again, mountain areas figure prominently in the Japanese system of national parks. As Fig. 9.13 illustrates, two-thirds of these are in the uplands, while the rest are made up of islands and coasts. Japan's highly irregular coastline, with its many rocky headlands and its countless offshore islands, offers some very beautiful scenery (see Fig. 9.14).

Fig. 9.12 *Hot spring resort*

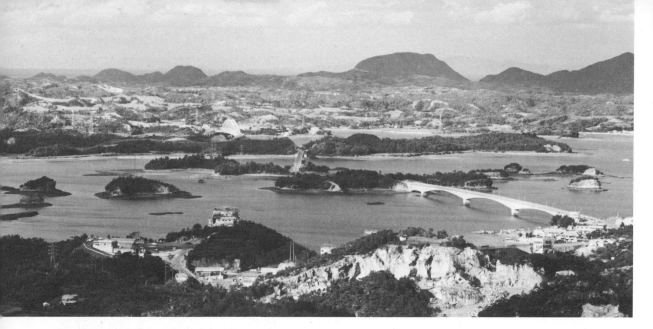

Fig. 9.14 *Island scenery*

One of the most photographed landscapes in all Japan is here at Matsushima, near the city of Sendai. The blue of the sea contrasts with the light-coloured rock of the islands and with the dark green of the wind-twisted pines which cover the rocks. There are, of course, some national parks (such as Saikai or Rishiri) where both volcanic mountains and coastal scenery are combined.

Water is in itself another natural leisure resource. Japan's lakes and waterfalls, which are found mainly in the uplands, add to the attractiveness of these areas for Japanese holiday-makers. To illustrate this, we can look more closely at the Hakone district, about 90 kilometres south-west of Tokyo. As Fig. 9.15 indicates, Lake Ashi is the centre-piece of this tourist area. The lake lies in an old volcanic crater, and is surrounded by conical lava mountains. Along the wooded shoreline of Lake Ashi are picnic grounds, camp-sites and golf courses, while the lake itself is used for swimming, boating and fishing. The Sukumo and Hayakawa Rivers, which drain away from the lake area, have cut steep narrow valleys which add to the beauty of the landscape. Since the district, like so much of Japan, still has volcanic activity, there are also several busy hot spring resorts.

In Japan, perhaps more than anywhere else, trees and flowers play a vital part as a tourist resource. Every month has its own recognised plants, and every traditional beauty spot has its own distinctive mixture of vegetation. Shinto shrines, for example, often have coniferous trees as symbols of good fortune and endurance. Lotus blossoms, standing for purity, grow in pools beside Buddhist temples.

Seasonal changes are another special attraction. In spring, bus-loads of visitors come to view the cherry blossom at traditional sites, such as Sakurayama or Yoshinoyama. The short-lived cherry flower is a reminder for the Japanese of the quick passing of human life. In autumn, thousands of countryside visitors admire the red, gold and brown leaves of maple and elm trees, seen against the dark green of cedar and cypress. The natural vegetation of Japan is protected, not only in the zones shown in Fig. 9.13, but also in the 54 Quasi-National Parks looked after by the Enviroment Agency, and in the 249 other areas registered as prefectural parks.

Historical areas

Japan, as we have already seen, has two

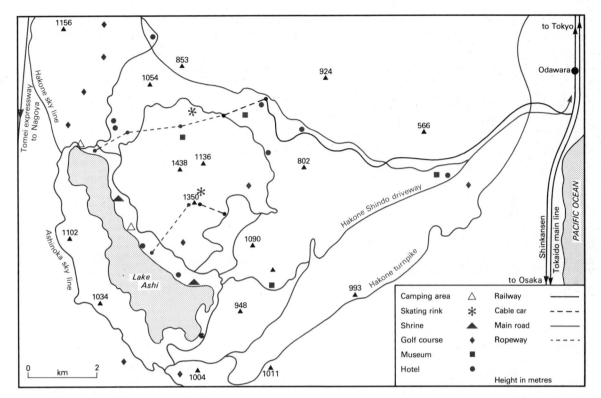

Fig. 9.15 *Lake Hakone tourist area*

main religions. Shinto is the older, and has close ties with the physical geography of the country. Its shrines are built in places where some legendary event occurred or where some spirit of nature is supposed to reside. Shinto tradition links high places with divine spirits, and thus many sacred buildings appear on mountain slopes. In the same way, climbing Mount Fuji to view the early sunrise from its summit is a favour-

Fig. 9.16(a) *Climbing Mount Fuji with bicycle;* **(b)** *Japanese postage stamp featuring Mount Fuji*

ite form of pilgrimage (see Fig. 9.16) Amidst the vast collection of Shinto spirits, the chief is the Sun Goddess, Amaterasu, who has her main shrine at Ise. (Fig. 11.4) This is perhaps the most holy place in the whole of Japan, and is therefore the scene of year-round tourism. All Shinto shrines (Fig. 9.17) are arranged in ranks, ranging from tiny roadside structures to huge enclosures which draw visitors from every corner of the country.

Buddhism came into Japan from China during the sixth century, and many new ideas were adopted around that time. Great wooden temples were erected in a number of places, especially round about the old capital cities of Nara and Kyoto. Several still stand and are therefore among the oldest timber buildings in existence anywhere. These ancient temples, along with the gigantic statues of Buddha at Nara and Kamakura, are major tourist attractions. Also dating from medieval times are Japan's great castles (see Fig. 1.15) The feudal lords who once ruled over areas of the Japanese country-side build multi-storied fortresses. Some of these have survived, and are now important tourist venues, partly because of their historical interest and partly for their art treasures, including priceless paintings and superbly decorated wood-work.

However, not all of the historic sites date as far back as the medieval period. Some are more modern. The east coast town of Shimoda, for instance, is where ships from the United States first made contact with Japan in 1854. Then again, Hiroshima's Peace Memorial Park and Nagasaki's Statue of Peace mark the only two spots where atomic bombs have ever exploded in war-time. Millions of Japanese and overseas tourists visit these sites every year.

We have been looking at patterns of scenic and historic tourism in Japan. What also has to be remembered is that the two forms are usually combined.

Major urban attractions

The central areas of the biggest Japanese

Fig. 9.17 *The torii gate of the Shinto shrine at Miyajima on the Inland Sea, near Hiroshima*

always less than the outward movement of Japanese tourists going abroad.

Foreign holidays

The Japanese have become, like the Americans, notable world travellers (Fig. 9.19). Although the majority still holiday in their own country, during the past few years an annual average of over three million Japanese have been going on visits abroad. By far the most popular areas for overseas tourism are those, such as Taiwan, South Korea and the Philippines, which can be reached most easily from airports in Japan. The United States (especially California) is also an important destination for Japanese visitors, because the two countries have had close links ever since the American Occupation (1945–52). Certain islands in the Pacific, such as Guam and Hawaii, are also fairly convenient for Japanese tourists, as are the cities of South-East Asia, such as Singapore and Bangkok. One other area deserves mention. Japanese visitors in large numbers nowadays make the long journey to the capitals of Western Europe, where they can find a very different culture from their own.

Fig. 9.18 *The Great Buddha of Kamakura*

cities act in their own right as strong tourist attractions. Huge department stores and great museums, for example, help to draw in visitors from a wide hinterland. Tokyo, above all, has special features such as the Imperial Palace (Fig. 9.18), the Ginza shopping quarter and the high look-out platforms on the Tokyo Tower. These are permanent points of interest, of course, but Japanese cities have also been the scene of very important temporary features. Thus, Tokyo was the site of the 1964 Olympic Games, while Osaka held the giant international exhibition known as Expo '70, and the Winter Olympics of 1972 were held at Sapporo. The result is that Japan, over the past twenty years, has been visited by many millions of foreigners. Yet, the inwards flow of visitors during any year is

Fig. 9.19 *Overseas destinations of Japanese travellers, 1982*

	Country	Total travellers
1.	United States	1,447,000
	(Incl. Guam :	264,440
	Hawaii :	718,000
2.	Taiwan	579,507
3.	South Korea	518,013
4.	Hong Kong	515,697
5.	Singapore	378,501
6.	West Germany	348,346
7.	Italy	303,485
8.	Switzerland	244,444
9.	United Kingdom (1979)	220,400
10.	Macao	168,955

Total travellers worldwide (1983) 4,232,000

Transport Networks

Introduction

Movement is very much a part of everyday life in Japan. People and goods are always on the move somewhere in the country, along transport lines or routes. Some of these, such as roads and railways, are visible features in the landscape. Others, like the routes followed by ships and aircraft, are not visible, although they can be drawn as lines or networks on maps. It is these road, rail, air and sea networks which we shall be studying in the present chapter.

Roads

Until the past fifty years or so, it was difficult to make the long journey from one end of Japan to another. Narrow, winding roads followed both the Pacific and Japan Sea coastlines, while other trackways through upland passes joined the coastal roads. The first real improvements came in the years between 1603 and 1868. Once Japan had been unified under a single ruler, with Edo, the forerunner of modern Tokyo, as the centre of government, there was a constant flow of traffic along the Tokaido road, between the new centre and the old capital, Kyoto.

Most of the movement was on foot, or occasionally on horseback, and travellers still had many rivers to ford, at great risk to themselves. When wheeled vehicles first came into widespread use after the middle of the nineteenth century, they were restricted to areas around the main cities. Then, during the American Occupation of 1945–52, passenger coaches and goods vehicles came into wider use, although they still had to travel on rough, unsurfaced roads throughout much of the country. By this time, a clear contrast could be seen between the better quality roads of the Tokaido urban area and the poorer roads in the rest of Japan. The differences were caused by two major factors.

1. Physical

Roads are cheaper to build in countryside which is more or less level. Thus, the mountainous backbone of Honshu, especially in the north, has a very limited network of good roads, and unsurfaced farm tracks are still the rule. By contrast, the road network in and between the main east coast cities is clearly first class (see Fig. 10.1).

2. Economic

Roads are built where there is an obvious demand for them, and in Japan the demand has always been greatest along the line of the Tokaido megalopolis, between Tokyo and Kyoto-Osaka. Over the past thirty years, car ownership has steadily increased (Fig. 10.2). The numbers of people using other means of transport have meantime been decreasing. To cope with the vast number of vehicles now in use, the Japanese road system has had to be extended and improved (Fig. 10.3).

The growth in road traffic has also produced problems of noise and air pollution. Yet, whatever its drawbacks, the road network is by far the most important method of moving people and light cargo throughout the country, because it allows

Fig. 10.1 *The Tomei expressway (Tokyo-Nagoya) at the Lake Hamana service area*

vehicles to reach all sorts of destinations, including homes, shops, factories and farms. Other networks, such as rail, sea and air, simply cannot do this.

Rail

The first railways in Japan were constructed during the 1870s, and a nationwide network gradually developed. It included trunk lines along the Pacific and Japan Sea coasts, with subsidiary lines joining the two. In 1906, the main network was nationalised, continuing till now as the state-run Japan National Railways (Fig. 10.4). For a long time, the JNR was successful. When the motor vehicle was first introduced, the Japanese paid it little attention. They relied instead on the railway, which did after all move people and freight more quickly and reliably than any other method.

In addition to the main lines, privately-owned suburban networks also grew up around the major cities. A tradition of commuting by rail to work thus developed, and continues strongly to this day. The six largest cities also have the advantage of subway systems, which, like the London Underground carry especially heavy commuter traffic.

Fig. 10.2 *Passenger and freight traffic*

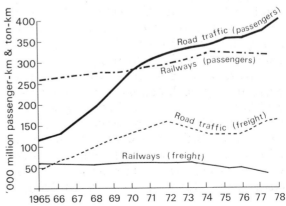

FY	Length of paved roads (km)	No. vehicles on road ('000 vehicles)
1954	9,279	763
1955	9,897	870
1956	11,445	1,008
1957	12,786	1,182
1958	14,327	1,379
1959	16,185	1,672
1960	17,447	2,082
1961	19,813	2,667
1962	23,015	3,433
1963	26,687	4,369
1964	30,490	5,468
1965	36,737	6,641
1966	45,363	8,044
1967	53,317	9,896
1968	61,549	12,145
1969	71,341	14,586
1970	82,453	17,012
1971	93,190	19,325
1972	102,521	21,788
1973	111,985	24,158
1974	118,578	26,151
1975	125,950	28,229

Fig. 10.3 *Road building [Note: The 1982 figures are Road Length – incl. local roads 175,514; Vehicles on road (1983) 42,619]*

During the past twenty years, the main improvement in the railway system has been the creation of a high speed train network, known as the *Shinkansen* or '*hikari*' (meaning bullet). Running from Tokyo southwards into Kyushu and northwards to the far tip of Honshu, the Shinkansen (Fig. 10.5) averages 170 kilometres per hour; a speed which few railways in the world can match.

Yet, despite these improvements, the railway system has obviously been declining. Road vehicles can take people and goods direct from door to door, and this is an advantage which rail can never offer. Car owners, too, if they can find somewhere to park, often prefer driving to work rather than travelling in over-crowded trains. Thus, in 1955, for example, private cars took only two per cent of all the passenger-kilometres travelled in Japan, but by 1975 the figure was up to 35 per cent. As a result, while the busy inter-city and suburban lines still make a profit, the vast majority of railway lines are loss-makers. The JNR, paying out large sums for new investment, while seeing a dramatic fall-off of freight traffic, has become heavily burdened with debt. (The proportion of total freight traffic carried by JNR fell from 52% in 1955 to 8% in 1981.) In all likelihood, Japan will follow other industrial countries in closing down more of its remote and uneconomic railway lines.

Network measurements

Modern Japan has complicated road and rail networks, which differ from one part of the country to another. To measure these differences, we first

Fig. 10.5 *Shinkansen passing by Mount Fuji*

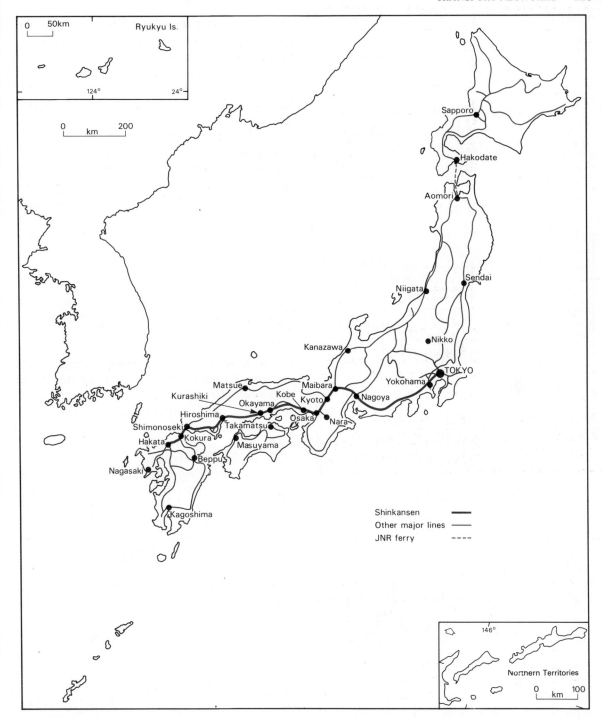

Fig. 10.4 *Rail network*

transform selected parts of the transport
network into manageable shapes. We can
do this by straightening out routes, to
form *edges*, and by putting in *nodes*
wherever there are settlements and route
junctions (see Fig. 10.6). The result is
known as a topological diagram, from
which we can carry out some simple cal-

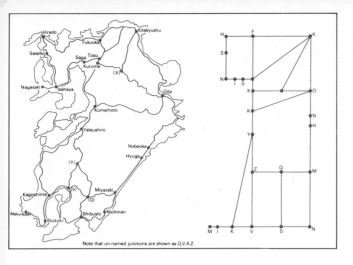

Note that un-named junctions are shown as Q,V,X,Z.

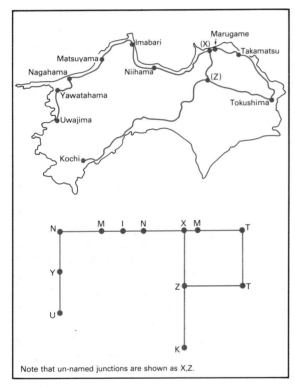

Note that un-named junctions are shown as X,Z.

Fig. 10.6 *Network examples*

there is at least one complete circuit in the network, while a value smaller than 1.0 indicates an incomplete network. The two factors most likely to affect the layout of any network, and hence its Beta Index, are relief and economics, which were referred to earlier.

Detours

Some networks, like the system of air routes within Japan, follow mainly straight lines. However, other networks are far less direct. The mountains of Japan and its irregular coastline act as barriers to the building of long straight stretches of road or railway. Hence, most journeys involve a detour of some kind. The Detour Index is used to measure how direct a journey is. It can be worked out as follows:

$$\frac{\text{actual distance travelled}}{\text{straight line distance}} \times \frac{100}{1}.$$

A detour index of 100 would indicate a journey which was as direct as possible. However, direct journeys are not the rule in Japan, and indices of 200 would be common in upland areas. Road journeys with high detour indices usually have other problems. Upland roads are not only winding. They are often narrow, with poor surfaces, so that overtaking is difficult and travel speed is low. Detours, in some cases at least, can be overcome. For many years now, there have been plans to construct a bridge or tunnel across the mouth of Tokyo Bay, to let travellers go from one side of the bay to the other,

Fig. 10.7 *Bridges of the Inland Sea*

culations. The first step is to compare the efficiency of any two networks. An efficient network is one which is well connected, and which therefore has a large number of edges in relation to nodes. An easy way of showing this is by calculating the Beta Index

$$= \frac{\text{number of edges}}{\text{number of nodes}} \text{ or } \frac{e}{n}.$$

Any index greater than 1.0 shows that

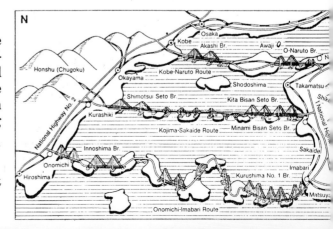

Fig. 10.8 *Omishima Bridge, completed 1979. (Length of span 297 metres)*

without going through central Tokyo. In the same way, the isolated position of the island of Shikoku will be largely overcome when the planned bridge system (Fig. 10.7) across the Inland Sea has been completed (Fig. 10.8).

the weight carried and the money earned). At the same time, the growth in air traffic meant that a new international airport had to be created at Narita, to the east of Tokyo. The problems associated with that development are dealt with in detail in Chapter 12.

Air

Air travel is important to Japan for several reasons. Anyone wanting to travel quickly from one of the small offshore islands to a large city like Tokyo or Sapporo would have to go by air (Fig. 10.9). In the same way, a traveller wanting to go from a town at one end of the country to a town at the other end, in the shortest possible time, might well choose air travel. For people going abroad from Japan on business or holiday, air is usually the only means of transport available.

The fact is that Japan has become ever more air-minded. Where only 5.2 million passengers flew on domestic routes within Japan during 1965, the number had risen to 40.9 million by 1980. JAL, (Japan Air Lines) the main Japanese airline, had by then become one of the world's busiest international passenger carriers (Fig. 10.10); in fact in 1984 the International Air Transport Association (IATA) declared JAL the world's number one airline (based on the distance flown,

Ports

As we have already seen, in Chapter 3, Japan is a nation with a strong maritime tradition. However, its merchant fleet was largely destroyed in World War II, and for some years afterwards there were severe restrictions on shipbuilding in Japan. From 1950 onwards, while national imports and exports began to grow year by year, Japanese shipyards started to build a new merchant fleet. By 1980, it was the second largest on the world's oceans (Fig. 10.11), although the greater part of Japan's overseas cargo transport was still carried by foreign ships.

Meanwhile, about a quarter of all the goods handled in Japanese ports is coastal traffic. In a country which is broken up into separate islands, coastal shipping will always be an essential lifeline, particularly for bulky goods like oil, coal, ore and timber.

Over the years, a contrast has developed between ports on the Pacific coast and those on the Japan Sea side of the country. The Japan Sea coast is

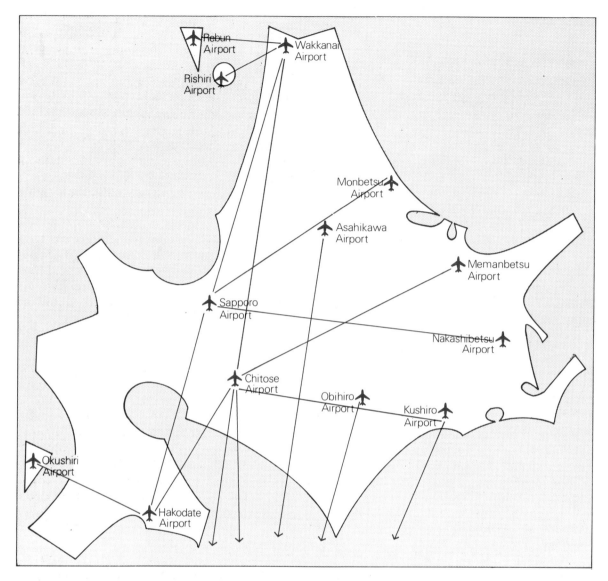

Fig. 10.9 *Air routes: Hokkaido*

Fig. 10.10 *A Japan Air Lines 747 at Haneda Airport, Tokyo*

sometimes described as blind, because it has few openings to the outside world. (Niigata, one of the major ports for trade between Japan and the USSR, is one of them.) On the other hand, the Pacific side is lined with ocean gateways, through which imports and exports pass in a ceaseless flow. Japan's hundreds of ports can also be classified by size into four main groups, as Fig. 10.12 shows. The major international ports are located in the main cities, which are also leading centres of manufacturing. Ranking below

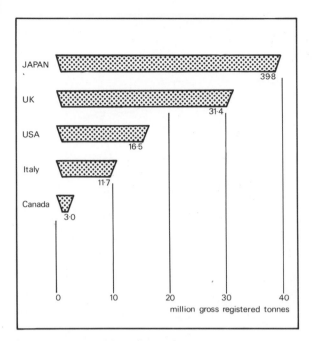

Fig. 10.11   *Merchant fleets by country (1978)*

3. Deepwater channels have been created by dredging, so that large ships can have better access to new and existing ports.

4. Adjacent to deepwater channels, new land has been created for industry and cargo handling. Modern industry in Japan has in most cases grown close to the coast. One advantage of this is that bulky cargoes do not have to be carried inland, but a disadvantage is that new land for industrial expansion has to be reclaimed from the sea, at enormous expense.

As an example of recent changes in a major Japanese port, a case study of Kobe follows.

Case study - Kobe

Although Kobe has only grown into a large city during the past hundred years, in that time it has also become one of the world's leading ports. In size, Kobe is overshadowed by its neighbour, Osaka. But, where Osaka city dominates its port, in Kobe it is around the port that the city is organised. Main roads run parallel to the waterfront, while other shorter roads cut across these, only to be stopped short by the nearby hills. At every intersection, there is a view of the harbour and all its activity.

As a port, Kobe has the advantages of a deepwater bay, sheltered from the open Pacific, plus excellent road and rail links with other major cities in Japan. On the other hand, it has the drawback of being built on a very restricted site, with steep hills forcing the city into a narrow coastal strip, only two kilometres wide but over

these there is a vast range of officially recognised ports of varying size.

Since ports are so vital to the economy of Japan, ever since 1961, there has been, a series of five-year plans for port development. This development has taken four different forms.

1. New ports have been created, to handle cargoes arriving in recently developed industrial regions of Japan. An example (Fig. 10.13) is the modern petroleum terminal at Kiire, on Kagoshima Bay in southern Kyushu.

2. Breakwaters have been constructed, to enlarge the area of several existing ports, such as Nagoya and Yokkaichi. Inside these breakwaters, ships can lie at anchor, sheltered from typhoons and winter blizzards.

Fig. 10.12   *Classification of Japanese ports*

Major international ports (5)		Yokohama, Kobe, Tokyo, Osaka, Nagoya
International ports (12)	e.g.	Nagasaki, Chiba, Shimizu, Kawasaki
Major Ports (94)	e.g.	Hakodate, Kashima, Hiroshima, Niigata
Loal ports (over 900)	e.g.	Imabari, Nemuto, Hamada, Funakawa

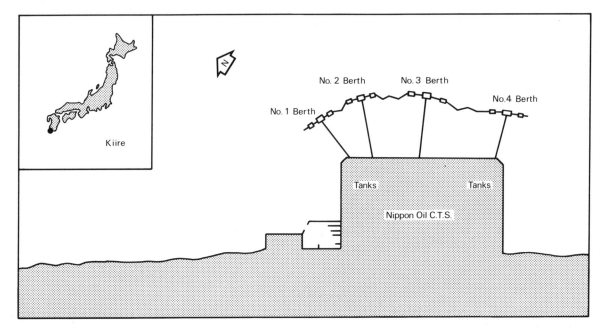

Fig. 10.13 *Kiire Port*

thirty kilometres long. To a large extent, the story of Kobe port is a story of extending the site by reclamation.

In the years between 1854, when Japan was first opened again to foreign trade, and 1940, blocks of new land were reclaimed from the bay for port industries, such as steel making and marine engineering. In addition, piers were constructed to give extra space for cargo handling

Fig. 10.14 *Kobe: Maya Piers, completed 1967*

Fig. 10.15   *Kobe: Part or Port Island container terminal — the largest in the world*

(Fig. 10.14). Yet these new facilities simply did not provide enough room for Kobe's growing trade. So, from 1953 onwards, a new phase of land reclamation began. This has added a large number of new piers and stretches of industrial land on both sides of the city centre.

Eventually, the entire waterfront was fully occupied. Kobe city authority then approached the Japanese government for help, under the third national port plan. Thus, in 1966, work started on a large artificial island in the middle of the harbour. To construct this island, the eroded hills behind Kobe had to be quarried. Millions of tonnes of sandy debris were brought out by an elevated conveyor belt, leading down to Suma Harbour. From there, barges carried the material into mid-harbour, where a rectangular embankment was built. Then, the space enclosed within the embankment

was gradually filled in. Unfortunately, the transport of rock debris made the waters of the bay even more muddy than they had been before. Another undesirable result was the removal of woodland which had protected the steep hills on the north side of the city. However, the denuded slopes have now been partly occupied by modern housing estates, which do at least ease some of the pressure on the crowded city below.

The product of years of reclamation was *Port Island*. Today, it is lined with quays for container ships (Fig. 10.15) and cargo liners. Its interior is taken up by offices and large concrete residential blocks, housing over 20,000 inhabitants. The island is linked to the city by a red-painted arch bridge, carrying vehicle traffic on two decks, along with an electric railway, which puts the island within ten minutes travel from central Kobe. Port

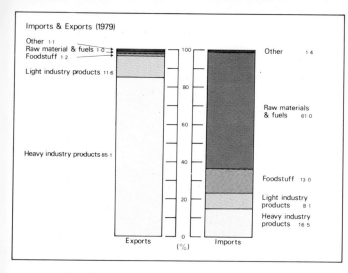

Other 1·1
Raw material & fuels 1·0
Foodstuff 1·2

Light industry products 11·6

Heavy industry products 85·1

Exports

(%)

Other 1·4

Raw materials & fuels 61·0

Foodstuff 13·0

Light industry products 8·1

Heavy industry products 16·5

Imports

Fig. 10.16 *Imports and exports (1979)*

even larger than Port Island, was begun in 1972, and by 1983 its new surface was partly built up. It, too, has container berths, a terminal for car exports and a ferry terminal. All of this modern construction has changed the face of Kobe port, and the former shortage of space has been overcome, despite the costs involved. Other Japanese ports have adopted the same technique. For example, Osaka, Nagoya and Tokyo have all added to their harbour areas by winning land from the sea.

Trade

Throughout the world, Japan is a major trader and its pattern of trade has several distinct features.

1. Japanese trade reached its present

Island was completely reclaimed by 1975, and by 1983 (Fig. 10.17) it had been fully developed.

Meanwhile, just two kilometres to the east, another block of artificial land was created in Kobe Harbour. Rokko Island,

Fig. 10.17 *Housing and exhibition area at Port Island, Kobe*

high level by increasing rapidly during the 1960s and 1970s. Between 1967 and 1977, for instance, it grew sevenfold. However, the rate of increase has slowed down in more recent years.

2. Since 1973, Japan has been the third major trading nation, after the USA and West Germany. This has led some people to wrongly imagine that Japan produces goods mainly for export. Yet, Japanese exports in 1980 were worth only one-eighth of the value of all goods and services produced in the country during that year. In fact, the best customers for Japanese goods are the Japanese themselves.

3. Japan is an exporter of manufactured goods and an importer of foods and raw materials, as Fig. 10.16 indicates. This pattern does not stay unchanged over the years, however. It seems, for example, that there will be little further increase in raw materials imports for the steel and heavy chemicals industries, which have already reached their upper limit of output. On the export side, meantime, Japanese products are ever more likely to be high-value, low-volume goods, rather than the bulky products (like steel, ships or plastics) which have been important in the past.

4. Japan has a group of close partners in trade. The best buyers of Japanese goods are the USA, certain European countries (including Britain and West Germany) and a number of Asian states (such as China, Taiwan, South Korea, Hong Kong and Singapore). To these customers, Japan sends a massive outflow of vehicles, mechanical equipment and electrical products. At the same time, Japan itself is a major buyer of oil, ore, timber and grain. Its main suppliers of these raw materials are Australia, Canada, the USA and the nations of the Arabian Gulf.

5. A number of problems have been created by Japan's present trade pattern. One of these is imbalance, whereby some European countries spend vast sums on imports from Japan, only to find that Japan buys little in return. European governments sometimes retaliate by setting limits on how much they will import from Japan in any one year.

A different source of worry is Japan's dependence on nations like Iran, Saudi Arabia and Kuwait for essential supplies of crude oil. These supplies could be blocked by armed conflict in the Arabian Gulf, and the result would be economic disaster for Japan.

Although most of Japan's manufactures are used within the country itself, Japan has also done well out of foreign trade. Many of its raw materials are bought quite cheaply from poor countries, while its finished products are sold more widely in the rich countries than in the poor. At the same time, Japan has learned that trade makes nations dependent on each other.

As we saw earlier (in Chapter 6), there is always a danger that trade barriers might prevent Japanese goods from gaining entry to any one of the other industrial nations. For that reason, Japan has been setting up branch factories in Britain, Eire and Singapore, for example. Clearly, there can be no barrier against locally manufactured articles, even if the factory producing them is Japanese-owned.

Trade barriers can be overcome in other ways. For instance, a number of overseas companies, admitting their own lack of success in competing against Japan, have paid Japanese firms for manufacturing licences. These licences allow the overseas firms to assemble goods, using components from Japan. Trade, therefore, in all its different forms, has enabled the title *Made in Japan* to spread all over the world.

11 Urban Patterns

The growth of towns and cities

Modern Japan is a nation of town dwellers. More than that, it is a nation of *large* towns, since by 1975 more than two-thirds of the population were living in places with over 50,000 inhabitants. But towns and cities have not always been so important in the life of Japan. For one thing, Japanese cities are not particularly old by world standards. Cities in other countries, like Alexandria in Egypt, Athens in Greece or Canton in China, are many centuries older than any in Japan. Indeed, it was not until the eighth century that Japan's existing cities first appeared. They were built for a number of different reasons.

Fig. 11.1 *Planned layout of ancient Kyoto*

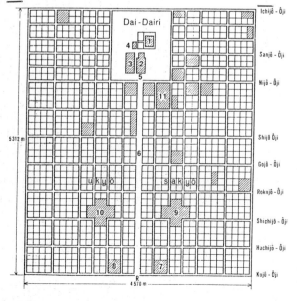

1. *Capital cities*

During the first few centuries A.D., Japan was divided up among many clans, each with its own territory and leader. In 645, however, members of one family living near the centre of the country were recognised as the Imperial rulers. In 715 A.D. a capital city was planned for them on very grand lines, with enormous avenues, criss-crossing to form a grid plan. This first city, Nara, lasted only 70 years as a capital, to be replaced by Kyoto. It, too, was laid out in rectangular form, imitating the great cities of Ancient China (Fig. 11.1).

Today, Nara is a vast sprawl of old temple buildings, loosely connected by roads and residential areas. It is also the seat of the prefectural administration (Nara prefecture) and it contains universities as well as some manufacturing industries. Kyoto on the other hand has proved more durable. With its museums, craft workshops (Fig. 11.2), hotels and shopping arcades, it is today one of the outstanding tourist attractions in all Asia.

2. *Castle towns*

Throughout the Middle Ages, Japan was in a state of unrest, with one clan warring

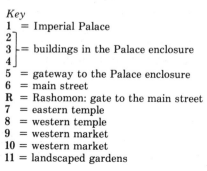

Key
1 = Imperial Palace
2
3 = buildings in the Palace enclosure
4
5 = gateway to the Palace enclosure
6 = main street
R = Rashomon: gate to the main street
7 = eastern temple
8 = western temple
9 = western market
10 = western market
11 = landscaped gardens

Fig. 11.2 *Craft workshop (woodblock printing) at the Kyoto Handicraft Centre*

facturing came to Japan in the nineteenth century, the castle towns were the places best able to take advantage of the new opportunities. A sure sign of their success is the fact that, out of today's 47 prefectural capitals, 33 were originally castle towns. Likewise, the main cities of

Fig. 11.3 *Kanazawa city, untouched by war-time air-raids, remains a major centre for arts and crafts*

against another. However, by the 1500s, certain warlords were making their territory more secure by building fortified castles in carefully chosen spots. A common type of site was a low hill, overlooking neighbouring lowlands. The modern city of Kanazawa (Fig. 11.3), for example, was just one of many to begin on such a site. Castle towns were constructed all over the country, from Kumamoto in the far south of Kyushu, to Sendai in the north of Honshu. As a rule, they had two features in common.

(a) A large proportion of the inhabitants (over half, in some cases) were warriors, whose living quarters made up the main outline of the town. The more important military men lived in the zone closest to the castle, while the rest lived further out.

(b) Every castle town had a number of merchants and craftsmen, living separately from the warriors, while supplying them with food and equipment. Each town also had its own priests and religious buildings, coming under the control of the ruling lord.

The castle town had the advantage that it could carry out several different tasks, such as trade, administration and craft industry. Thus, when modern manu-

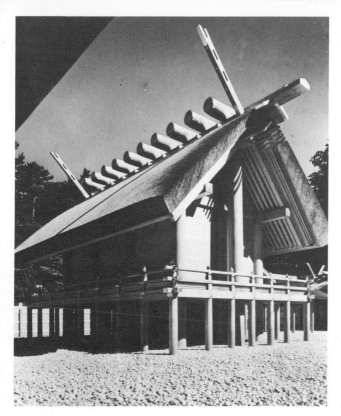

Fig. 11.4 *Shrine at Ise*

the Pacific coast, including Tokyo, Osaka, Nagoya and Hiroshima, all grew around a castle town core.

3. Religious centres

Buddhist temples and Shinto shrines, representing the two great religions of Japan, are scattered throughout the country. Some have special importance. For example, Ise (Fig. 11.4) is the holy place of the ancestor-goddess of the Japanese Royal family, while Izumo on the west coast is the other great sacred location of the Shinto belief.

Nara and Kyoto, the former capital cities, are surrounded by legendary sites and holy buildings. For centuries, it has been the custom for people to go on pilgrimages to these places, and the most popular religious centres have become modern tourist resorts, with large-scale shopping facilities.

4. Market towns

During the Middle Ages, weekly markets were held at various crossroads sites, all over the countryside of Japan. Over the centuries, a number of such places have taken on other functions, such as religion and craft industries, and have eventually become large cities. Yokkaichi and Shimonoseki are just two examples.

5. Resorts

Volcanic activity (see Chapter 2) is common in Japan. It produces, in its turn, hot springs, which people visit for health reasons. These hot spring resorts are scattered widely in Japan. Some have become satellites for larger cities, like Takarazuka for Osaka, while a few, like Beppu in Kyushu, are important enough to attract visitors from all over the country.

6. Ports

Japan had, even as early as the 1200s, a large urban population. These people, producing no food supplies of their own, needed large amounts of rice to stay alive. There was, therefore, a coastal trade in rice, from areas of surplus to the main cities. Each city had its own seaport for this purpose, and there were also a few chosen ports where foreign trade was allowed. Hyogo, the forerunner of modern Kobe, traded with China, as did its neighbour Sakai. Nagasaki, meanwhile, was the only seaport which had permission to trade with Europe.

Alongside these larger ports were hundreds of coastal fishing villages. A small number of these older places, such as Osaka and Sakai, have become modern port-cities, but many more Japanese ports are entirely twentieth-century creations.

7. Stage towns

The Japanese government, all through the period from 1603 to 1868, required noblemen and some of their retainers to spend alternate years living in Edo (modern Tokyo), where they would be under the eyes of the authorities. To reach Edo, most travellers would use one or

Fig. 11.5 *One of the '69 Stations of the Kisokaido' by Ikeda Eisen*

other of the five main roads leading to the capital from various corners of the country. (Fig. 11.5) The busiest of these roads was the Tokaido, referred to in Chapter 10.

At intervals along all the important roads, stage towns grew, offering facilities for the thousands of travellers, including nobles, servants, soldiers and pilgrims, who journeyed every week to

Fig. 11.6 *Interior and exterior of Japan's first spinning factory to apply mass-production techniques. Opened in 1872*

and from Edo. Every few miles, there was a cluster of inns, restaurants, stables, bath-houses, food stalls and barber shops. Nowadays, of course, travellers do not need so many services so closely spaced, and thus the majority of stage towns have remained small in size. A few, however, like Shimizu and Numazu, on the Tokaido route, have become large modern cities, but only because of their recent industrial development.

The phase of urban concentration

Once Japan was opened up to western ideas, towns became ever more important. Between 1868 and 1945, most towns grew in size, while taking on many new functions. The changes occurring during that period were mainly caused by three factors.

1. *Transport*

One of the most far-reaching changes to come about in Japan during the late 1800s

was the building of a nationwide railway network. Many of the old castle towns now became rail junctions or terminals. In the larger settlements, the main station had to be built some distance away from the already overcrowded city centre. Thus, a new urban sector quickly grew up, with its own shops, hotels and other services.

Railway development went hand-in-hand with the growth of certain resort towns and seaports. Kobe and Yokohama, for example, began their rise as major international ports at this time. In one entire region of Japan, urban growth was entirely dependent on new transport. The northern island of Hokkaido had been a backward area of uninhabited forests and mountain ranges, until the railway reached into northern Honshu, from which ferry steamers could take people across to Hokkaido.

2. Industry

With the help of foreign advisers and technicians, the Japanese began to adopt modern industry on a large scale after the 1860s. The first industries to grow were textiles and steel. Cotton mills were built, particularly around Osaka, where raw cotton was imported from China. Steel mills appeared in coastal locations, either close to coal, as at Yawata and Muroran, or close to iron ore, as at Kamaishi (refer back to Fig. 6.15). In every case, these huge new buildings (Fig. 11.6) looked completely different from anything which had previously existed in the Japanese urban landscape.

What is more important, the modern industries were setting a trend which is still very much in evidence: the preference of manufacturing firms for locating their factories on the coast. A different effect of industry was the growth of new manufacturing towns, in areas which had been entirely rural. Such towns were often controlled by one or other of the great industrial combines of Mitsui, Mitsubishi or Sumitomo.

Meanwhile, old-established industries, such as food and drink processing, together with the crafts of pottery, paper-making and carpentry, continued to exist in most Japanese towns. Their presence helped to ensure that the traditional appearance of these towns was at least partly preserved, well into the twentieth century.

3. Commerce

Long before modern industrial techniques were ever adopted in Japan, there was a strong tradition of well-organised craft industries. Skilled artisans produced high quality silk gowns, porcelain jars, lacquerware bowls and decorated swords, for example. Distributing and selling those craft products was carried out by merchants, who also brought up farm goods for re-sale to urban consumers. Merchants' shops and warehouses had therefore been part of the urban scene for many centuries.

The arrival of western ideas, however, meant that, after 1868, new building styles appeared in Japanese cities. Commercial offices and banks, for example, copied European and American fashions, as did other services, like hotels and department stores. The result of these many changes in transport, industry and commerce was to produce a townscape which was a curious mixture of traditional eastern buildings and more modern western ones (Fig. 11.7).

Reconstruction and change

Japanese cities have always been subject to extensive re-arrangement, following disastrous earthquakes or fires (see Chapter 12). However, the greatest factor ever to influence the shape of these cities was the American bombing campaign of

Fig. 11.7 *Kyoto Tower Hotel*

Fig. 11.8 *Hiroshima — after the atomic bomb, August 1945*

1944–45 (see Fig. 11.8). After the end of World War II, a massive programme of reconstruction began. While that was going ahead, Japan's manufacturing and service activities were also on the increase. Together, these changes had three major effects on towns and cities.

1. Industrial structures

Many of the early textile mills and metal smelting plants were either destroyed during the Pacific War, or were out of date by 1945. After that, for three decades, a seemingly endless series of new industries took over stretches of the Pacific coastline. The existing flatlands and the many blocks of recently reclaimed coastal land now house some of the world's largest industrial structures. Among them are, for example, the steel mills at Fukuyama and Wakayama, where tall chimneys, painted with red and white horizontal stripes, pour their waste gases into the skies (Fig. 11.9).

Around the three great bays at Tokyo, Osaka and Nagoya, huge box-like buildings, surrounded by towering chimneys, show where electrical power is produced for homes and factories. In these areas,

too, shiny steel tanks, globes and stacks mark the many sites of chemicals production. However, all industries do not gather on the waterfront.

On the inland side of most cities there are now industrial estates and individual factories, producing the lightweight electrical and optical goods in which Japanese companies are currently world leaders. These newer industries usually occupy two-storey blocks, and the companies often own nearby playgrounds, shops, clinics and housing (Fig. 11.10).

2. Suburban housing

An outstanding feature of Japanese urban areas over the past thirty years has been their outwards expansion into what used to be farmland. Suburban growth started soon after the end of World War II. Many townspeople had been left homeless by the war, while millions of country dwellers now wanted to take up new jobs in town. The only answer to this enormous demand was to build large apartment blocks (*danchi*) as quickly as possible (Fig. 11.11). Some were rented from the local authorities and many more were built by the Japan Housing Corporation, for sale or rent.

At first, these blocks were no more than four storeys high, since the Japanese

Fig. 11.9 *The tall chimneys of a modern industrial landscape*

Fig. 11.10 *Modern industrial estate*

had no tradition of high-rise dwellings. During the 1970s, however, the height of apartment blocks trebled, making them stand out clearly on the urban skyline. At the same time, more and more people were able to afford the very high prices asked for tiny new detached villas, and so this type of housing (Fig. 11.12) was soon spreading out on the fringes of Japanese cities.

Fig. 11.11 *Danchi*

3. *Central development*

It is in the central business districts of cities that some of the most spectacular changes have happened. For example, city centres have pushed outwards and upwards. Once buildings could be designed to withstand earth tremors, giant tower blocks became very evident (Fig. 11.13). Another important feature is *functional differentiation*.

Large CBDs, in cities throughout the world, tend to divide into sub-areas, each with its own special function. An example in Tokyo is Akihabara (Fig. 11.14) where, from hundreds of electrical discount stores, neon signs blaze and television sets blare. Just a few hundred metres to the south-west lies the Kanda bookshop district (Fig. 11.15), where one store might specialise in comics, another in dictionaries and another in Japanese history books, for students from the district's three universities.

Case study: Kanazawa

To sum up the changes affecting Japanese townscapes, we can look at the example of Kanazawa. The original town core is the castle, built by the Maeda clan in the

Fig. 11.12 *Modern detached villas*

Fig. 11.13 *High-rise office blocks*

1590s and still standing. Its grounds are now part of the campus of Kanazawa University. The lines of outer walls and moats which once protected the castle are now followed by modern streets.

In the inner city (Fig. 11.16) are a number of old-fashioned districts, once inhabited by warrior families serving the Maeda clan. In Cho, now re-named Nagamachi, the traditional timber houses remain, while the remnants of former canals can still be glimpsed and smelled in the deep gutters separating houses from the street. In these older districts, seafood, fruit and vegetables are sold in tiny shops which have been here for over three hundred years. Even the names of localities, like Stonecutters' Ward and Carpenters' Ward, belong to the past.

Beside the River Sai, meanwhile, the old religious buildings of Teramachi have fallen into partial disuse, as has the great temple of Kannon on the north side of the River Asano. Here, from the higher land, there is an excellent view across the city's

Fig. 11.14 *Akihabara electrical stores*

gleaming tile roofs, still as close-packed as they were centuries ago. Yet the forests of television aerials, telephone poles and power lines show that Kanazawa is much

Fig. 11.15 *Kanda bookshops*

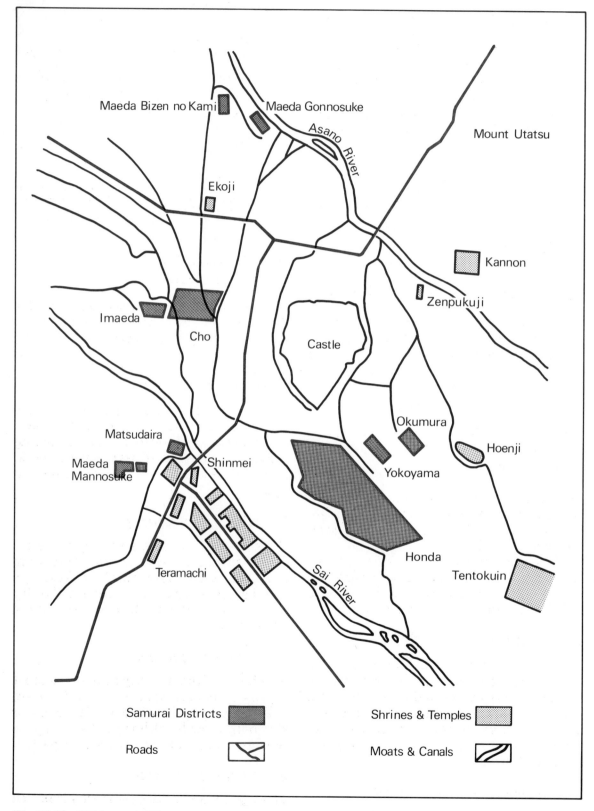

Fig. 11.16 *Old layout of Kanazawa*

more than just a living museum. So, too, on the old Hokuriku Highway, running diagonally across the city from north-east to south-west, it is hotels, garages, supermarkets and offices which line the road. Kanazawa, like many other old cities in Japan, has clearly moved with the times, while holding on to much of its past.

The shape of towns

As towns in Japan have grown throughout the years, each one has formed its own distinctive shape. Yet all towns have some features in common. Hence, rather than try to memorise the different layout of each town, geographers have made up models, to show the common features in the simplest possible way. In this section, therefore, we will consider three types of urban model. Before we do, there are three essential points to note.

1. *Towns are real*, while models are merely invented as aids to our understanding. Models, therefore, have to fit towns, but towns do not *have* to fit any particular model.

2. *Town shapes tend to be complex*, and we cannot, therefore, use one simple model to show how all towns are formed. Instead, we are likely to need more than one type of model.

3. *Every town is unique* in one way or another, and so we must always expect to find differences between urban models and the real towns which we study.

The concentric model

This idea, put forward by Burgess in the 1920s, suggests that, as a town grows, successive stages of building will form zones or rings, becoming newer towards the outer edge of town. Eventually, as many as five rings (see Fig. 11.17) will form, as follows.

1. The central business district

Being the most accessible part of town,

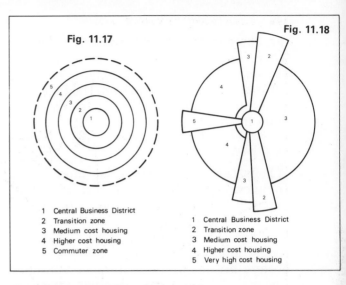

Fig. 11.17
Fig. 11.18

1 Central Business District
2 Transition zone
3 Medium cost housing
4 Higher cost housing
5 Commuter zone

1 Central Business District
2 Transition zone
3 Medium cost housing
4 Higher cost housing
5 Very high cost housing

Fig. 11.17 *Concentric urban model*

Fig. 11.18 *Sector model*

this central area is most suitable for shops, offices and other types of business. Very few people will actually live here, however.

2. The transition zone

This was once a densely populated zone, where the older buildings have often been demolished or renovated. The remaining homes are mixed with warehouses, workshops and retail stores of various sizes and ages.

3. Medium-cost housing

Houses in this zone are usually in better condition than those in the transition zone, and there is less crowding. Although land here is less expensive than in the city centre, the actual houses are more expensive.

4. Higher-cost housing

Still further from the city centre, the most expensive houses appear, where they are unlikely to be disturbed by factories or shopping crowds, although there may be schools nearby and the occasional park.

5. The commuter zone

These are communities separated from the main built-up area by open countryside, but connected to it by roads and railways. This zone can, therefore, include farmsteads, old villages and modern housing estates. It gets its name from the fact that many of its inhabitants travel to work daily in the city.

Applying the model

When the zones of this model are compared with those of real cities in Japan, the following differences are seen.

1. No city has complete zones encircling the centre. Barriers, such as rivers, hills, the coast and transport lines always break up the pattern of building. The model, by contrast, assumes a perfectly even surface stretching in all directions.

2. Buildings extend further out along main roads. In the model, meanwhile, routeways are not allowed for, and the zones are therefore regularly shaped.

3. The outer edge is not always high-cost housing, since part of it is usually occupied by local authority apartment blocks.

4. Many cities have an ancient core, surrounding a castle, and a later core around the main railway station. The presence of two centres makes it impossible for a perfect concentric pattern to form.

The sector model

This idea was first proposed by Homer Hoyt in the 1930s. Its most important feature is the area of high quality housing (Fig. 11.18) which tends to form in the most favoured part of the city. The attraction might be land with an open view, or land well away from noise and pollution. Whatever the basis, once high quality housing begins to expand, it does so within the sector where it first formed.

When this sector is fully established, it will tolerate few other land uses in its vicinity. Parks and other open spaces are a possibility, but factories, warehouses and poor quality housing are not. These other uses tend to gather towards the opposite sector of the city. The area between the two extremes will be occupied by medium quality housing. Meanwhile, the city centre will be the main focus for all types of business.

Applying the model

When this model is compared with the layout of Japanese cities, one major difference is obvious. The contrast between high quality and low quality housing is generally not as marked in Japan as it might be in North America or Western Europe. In fact, pockets of expensive housing would be found in many different sectors of any Japanese city, side by side with poorer homes. What is more, the outward differences between richer and poorer areas of Japanese cities are, by international standards, not at all striking. Even the very wealthy in Japan would not, for example, own houses with twenty bedrooms, swimming pools and tennis courts, as their counterparts in other countries might do.

The multiple nuclei model

Yet another model of urban structure is

Fig. 11.19 *Multiple nuclei model*

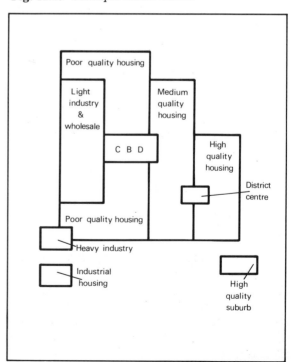

Fig. 11.20 *Tsuru city new town, Yamanashi Prefecture*

based on the idea that different land uses such as shopping, housing and industry usually grow up in their own separate areas. As time goes on, and the intervening spaces become built upon, so the various original nuclei will eventually merge into a single pattern (Fig. 11.19), just as do the zones and sectors which we saw in earlier models.

This model, then, suggests that different land uses need to grow separately. Some uses, such as business and transport, prefer city centres, where they can be accessible to their customers. By contrast, high quality housing will be repelled by noise, crowding and pollution, and will therefore expand on the edge of town, where these problems are least evident. This model is useful for Japanese cities which have grown large enough to swallow up nearby towns, and which then include these settlements as multiple nuclei within the overall urban pattern.

Urban problems and solutions

Whatever their shape, Japanese cities have grown rapidly during the period 1950–80. Growth has brought problems, as we shall see again in Chapter 12. For the present, however, we can look at some of the solutions which the Japanese have adopted for their urban problems.

1. *Decay and congestion*

In large cities all over the world, there are older areas, with buildings in poor condition, where the poor and the unemployed live. Vandalism, crime, addiction and family breakdown are more common there than in other parts of cities. It is important to notice that Japan is less affected by these problems than most other industrial nations. Urban decay is not especially widespread, since so many buildings date from the post-war period. On the other hand, congestion has been an extremely serious problem, for which several different solutions have been tried.

First, as we saw earlier in this chapter, *danchi* were built on an extensive scale. Yet this solution has created its own difficulties. These apartments are mainly inhabited by wage earners aged between thirty and forty. Wives complain of isolation while husbands are at work and children at school. The old Japanese extended family, with grandparents living in with their married children, has little place in these modern homes. Equally, the sense of community which was traditionally strong in the older urban areas is unlikely to develop in the *danchi*, where neighbours may not even know each other.

A second solution to the problem of congestion is the construction of new towns (Fig. 11.20). Tsukuba, for example, was built during the 1970s as an academic city, to house over forty research facilities which moved out from Tokyo. Tama new town, on the other hand, was created simply to take surplus population from Tokyo. Meanwhile, other new towns were built near Osaka and Nagoya, where population was spilling out gradually from the most congested inner districts (Fig. 11.21).

The new towns clearly provide a safe and pleasant environment for young families, but they do have two major drawbacks. The initial cost of constructing them is high, and they offer limited opportunities for work. Thus, many of the new town dwellers commute to jobs in the

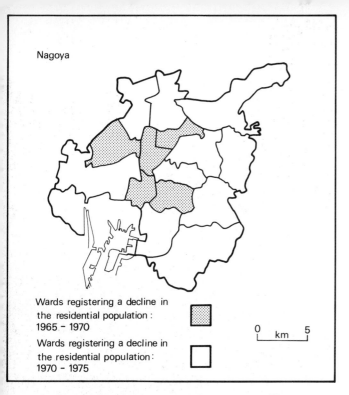

Wards registering a decline in
the residential population:
1965 - 1970

Wards registering a decline in
the residential population:
1970 - 1975

0   km   5

Fig. 11.21 *Population decline in inner Nagoya*

city from which they originally moved
house.

2. *Traffic*

Large Japanese cities suffer from acute
congestion, as thousands of commuters
travel in and out by road and rail each day
(Fig. 11.22). As car ownership increased
sharply after 1960, drivers found ever
greater difficulty in parking on or moving
through the narrow streets of old-
fashioned urban areas. At the same time,
slow-moving traffic caused serious air
pollution, and conditions for the average
pedestrian became hardly bearable.

There have been many different at-
tempts to ease the problems of traffic.
Some measures are designed to assist the
motorist. For example, modern expressways, flyovers and interchanges take

Fig. 11.22 *Nagoya's commuting pattern*

- - - Boundary of the NMA

⟵ Net flows of over 10,000 commuters

- - - Net flows of over 5,000 commuters

◎ Cities receiving over 5,000 commuters
from at least one other city

○ Cities supplying a minimum of 5,000
commuters to at least one other city

0 _____ 20km

some of the pressure off the ordinary street system, while creating new noise problems when elevated traffic passes close to the windows of residential blocks.

By contrast, other measures are devised to inhibit the driver. Car parking spaces are severely restricted, while some busy streets have been converted into pedestrian precincts (Fig. 11.23). Strict regulations require lead-free petrol to be used in cars, and there are similarly strict standards set for the education of learner-drivers. However, these solutions cannot hide the fact that city streets in Japan, as in all the other advanced nations, can barely cope with their gigantic burden of traffic.

In all, Japanese cities present a truly staggering challenge to urban planners. On the credit side, they are for the most part wealthy and crime-free places, without either racial or religious ghettoes, or boarded-up slums. Despite that, they sprawl for mile after mile, in the most untidy manner imaginable. Crowded housing, a general lack of privacy, mass commuting and a decline in community spirit are just some of the urban problems which are still far from being solved by government intervention.

Fig. 11.23 *Pedestrian precinct for Sunday shoppers in central Tokyo*

12 Planning

Types of region

It is always difficult to govern millions of people, living in several large islands, from one central city. Thus, to make government easier, medieval Japan was divided into provinces, each of which was subdivided into districts, ruled over by a local lord. When Japan began to modernise in the late nineteenth century, a rather similar system was set up. As Fig. 12.1 shows, the main unit in the country's modern regional organisation is the *prefecture*. Each of the 47 prefectures (Fig. 12.2) has its own capital city, with its own elected assembly and various offices concerned with agriculture, industry and the environment within the prefecture.

Yet the prefectures are very much within the control of the central government in Tokyo. Thus, the work of the police and of teachers, for example, is directed from the capital city, where the central government provides most of the money for these and other essential activities. What is more, local officials, such as city mayors and prefectural governors, have to visit Tokyo frequently, to consult central government officials.

However, for many people in Japan, it is the town or village level of local government (see Fig. 12.1 again) which is most likely to affect their daily lives. Hence, in any typical town, the local authority has the responsibility for maintaining its own roads, providing health clinics, disposing of garbage, laying on drinking water and organising the fire service. But, at all levels of regional organisation, there are two serious problems which have been affecting the country during the past twenty years. One is overcrowding, while the other is depopulation.

Regional problems: overcrowding

Japan is not one great hive of constant activity. Far from it. There are mountainous areas which have never been inhabited, and there are uplands which have lost whatever population they once had. But, despite these variations, the fact is that nearly half of the population is packed into the three great urban areas of the Tokaido megalopolis, representing only nine per cent of the land surface of Japan. In other words, people and their activities are more heavily concentrated (Fig. 12.3) on the Pacific coast of Japan than in any other area of similar size

Fig. 12.1 *Types of region*

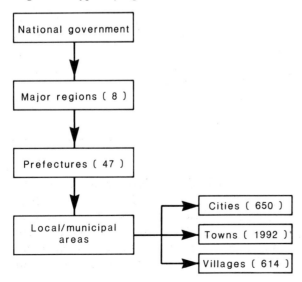

Fig. 12.2 *Prefectures*

Aichi	25	Miyazaki	45	Hyogo	17	Shimane	15
Akita	44	Miyagi	6	Ibaraki	39	Shizuoka	26
Aomori	45	Nagano	27	Ishikawa	30	Tochigi	39
Chiba	35	Nagasaki	3	Iwate	42	Tokushima	10
Ehime	8	Nara	20	Kagawa	9	Tokyo	34
Fukui	29	Niigata	32	Kagoshima	7	Tottori	16
Fukuoka	1	Oita	5	Kanagawa	33	Toyama	31
Fukushima	40	Okayama	14	Kochi	11	Wakayama	21
Gifu	24	Osaka	18	Kumamoto	4	Yamagata	43
Gumma	37	Saga	2	Kyoto	19	Yamaguchi	12
Hiroshima	13	Saitama	36	Mie	22	Yamanashi	28
Hokkaido	46	Shiga	23				

anywhere in the world. Extreme concentration on this scale leads to a number of difficulties, as we shall see.

1. *Sprawl*

As we saw in Chapter 1, the growth of large cities in Japan has produced urban areas which now stretch up to a hundred kilometres, from edge to edge. Beyond that edge, each main city has a huge cluster of commuter settlements, from which there is a vast daily flow of

Fig. 12.3 *Crowd scene: waiting for the bus in Nagoya*

Fig. 12.4 *Crowded urban park*

travellers to the central city.

2. Traffic congestion

Although most Japanese commuters travel by main-line railway and subway, large numbers do use private cars. So, like their counterparts in Europe or America, large cities in Japan suffer from congested roads and long traffic queues, as Chapter 11 has already described.

3. Lack of public amenities

Although the Japanese have on average become very much richer over the last twenty years, their city amenities do no always reflect this fact. Certainly, there are many glossy, tiled shopping plazas and luxury stores of every kind. But the narrow back streets, meanwhile, are poorly lit, and the smell of open drains

Prefecture	Percentage decline
Hokkaido	42.5
Aomori	9.6
Chiba	19.4
Kanagawa	30.0
Aichi	21.7
Mie	19.4
Shimane	23.2
Hiroshima	22.9
Kagoshima	28.9
Kochi	31.4

Fig. 12.5 *Population loss by rural areas of prefectures 1960-75*

hangs heavy in the air. Another drawback is that Japanese cities offer very few open spaces for the public to enjoy (Fig. 12.4).

4. *Public nuisance*

Every advanced nation has suffered some forms of pollution, or public nuisance, caused by the growth of industry. However, as Chapter 8 pointed out, Japan has experienced especially severe problems, for three main reasons.

(a) Industries kept expanding constantly over a number of years.

(b) Industries and all their pollutants are often crammed into restricted spaces, close to housing.

(c) For a long period, there were simply no adequate laws to protect the public from pollution.

Regional problems: depopulation

While extreme overcrowding is one kind of regional problem, depopulation is a completely different one. During the years between 1955 and 1970, for example, the countryside lost about ten million people to the towns and cities. As Fig. 12.5 indicates, rural prefectures in the far north and south of the country showed especially severe losses. However, even within one prefecture, the effects were not everywhere the same. Thus, all over the island of Hokkaido (Fig. 12.6), there were rural areas which were clearly losing population

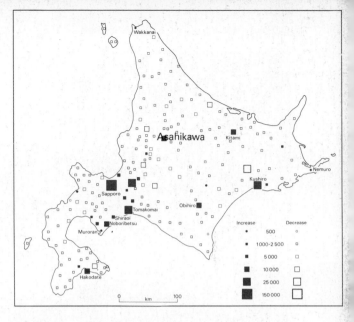

Fig. 12.6 *Population change in Hokkaido 1960-75*

during the late 1960s, while there were also areas in and around the main towns where population was growing.

The flood of people out of certain regions of Japan was caused on the one hand by *pull factors* – the attractions of urban life. Crowded though Japanese cities may be, they have offered a wide range of jobs, with generally high wages and all sorts of leisure-time activities. Equally well, the outwards migration of rural folk was also caused by various *push factors* – the unattractive aspects of country life.

Along the Japan Sea coast, for example, small communities are regularly cut off for days at a time by the massive midwinter snowdrifts. Medical help is hard to get in these conditions, and school attendance is equally difficult. Not surprisingly, many people look for somewhere else to live. In the same way, young country dwellers have been moving out from the far south of Kyushu, where very tiny farm holdings are traditional, and where careers in farming are not particularly attractive.

The results of these outwards movements have already been mentioned in Chapter 5. Large cities grow larger, while remote rural regions are left almost empty. What is important to notice is that these contrasts are likely to remain for a

Fig. 12.7 *A new bridge and tunnel under construction*

long time to come. Since the urban areas contain more than their share of young married people, it is in these areas that natural increase will go on during the years ahead. By contrast, the countryside, left with mainly older inhabitants, will be unable to replace those whom death removes.

Regional and local planning

The growing gulf between overcrowded and depopulated regions is just one of several long-term problems which government officials have to think about. Problems are found at all levels. At the national level, there has been widespread pollution of the environment, which can only be dealt with by nationwide laws and plans. Meanwhile, the national problem of an unevenly distributed population can only be dealt with by encouraging new growth in some regions, while discouraging it in others.

Regions can benefit, for example, from new motorways, road bridges and tunnels (Fig. 12.7). Again, there have to be plans to protect regions from the numerous natural hazards which affect Japan. At the local level, planned changes might include a renovated city centre or new extensions to a port. All three levels are important in a country which needs to plan for decent living standards, as well as for economic progress. We can look, therefore, at examples of each: Narita Airport at the local level, Hokkaido prefecture at the regional level, and large-scale development plans at the national level.

Case study – Narita Airport

We have already seen that it is hard to find room in Japan for large modern facilities, like port extensions or new industries. At the same time, a busy industrial nation needs a major international airport to handle its overseas traffic. A large airport, however, requires hundreds of hectares, to accomodate several runways, as well as large passenger halls, freight sheds and car parks.

Ever since the 1930s, Japan's main doorway to the air routes of the world has been Haneda Airport, on the south side of Tokyo. Although the site (Fig. 12.8) has good road and rail connections with the nearby city centre, it was not able to deal with the great expansion in air traffic during the 1970s. For one thing, the site is close to a heavily congested zone of factories and housing, where aircraft noise is a serious nuisance to thousands of local people. If the cramped site were extended south, new land would have to be reclaimed from Tokyo Bay, and the runways would then encroach on the busy shipping channel.

Similarly, to expand the airport in the other direction, into the densely packed urban area, was an equally unsuitable solution. Yet, Japanese trade was increasing rapidly at this time, and air connections with commercial centres in Australasia, North America and Western Europe were in great demand. Likewise, as the Japanese became generally richer, the demand for foreign holidays put further strains on the already crowded airport. Making the problem even worse was the common habit of visiting the airport to welcome friends arriving or to say farewell to those departing.

The only answer to the problems was to build on a completely new site, somewhere within one hour's travel from Tokyo. The first steps were taken in 1966, when the government chose a site at Narita, amidst the woods and farmlands of the Boso Peninsula, east of the capital. The site is large enough for an airport

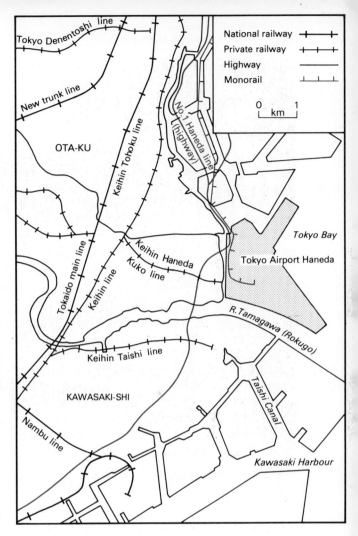

Fig. 12.8 *Location of Haneda Airport*

three times the size of Haneda (Fig. 12.9). Development here created thousands of new jobs in catering, cleaning and baggage handling. Outside the airport, many more jobs appeared in hotels, car hire and taxi firms, shops and banks.

On the other hand, the development at Narita caused a series of fresh problems.

1. *Noise*

People who had been accustomed to a peaceful rural life now had to put up with the overhead thunder of heavy jet aircraft.

2. *Transport costs*

The Narita site, sixty kilometres from central Tokyo, had to be made accessible to the city by building high quality expressways and a new railway link. These were costly improvements.

3. *Disturbance*

Over a thousand homes, on or beside the airport site, had to be given up. Again, hundreds of hectares of farmland had to be sold to the airport authority. Quite naturally, some farmers were angry at the loss of land which had, in some cases, been used for centuries by the same family.

4. *Public opposition*

Perhaps the most serious problem of all was caused by the way in which Narita was chosen. Local people argued that they had not been properly consulted, and there was little public discussion of the various costs and benefits of the project. However, Narita soon came to the attention of the public. Farmers, furious at the loss of their land, were joined by students protesting against the government's failure to discuss the scheme more openly.

The farmer-student alliance organised huge demonstrations, which ended in violent clashes with the police. During the 1970s, television news broadcasts all over the world showed ferocious battles at the Narita construction site, between riot police and armies of protesters. The final act was played out in 1978, when demonstrators wrecked the newly-completed airport control tower, despite the miles of heavy steel fencing put up to protect the site. The authorities replied by further strengthening the massive security screen. Heavily guarded by armed police, Narita was eventually opened in 1979 as the new international airport for Tokyo. (It should be noted, however, that because the student radicals chose Narita as their main base for confrontation, the demonstrations there were of a ferocity not repeated elsewhere in Japan where development schemes were also underway.)

Case study – Hokkaido

An example of a different solution to a different problem is the New Comprehensive Development Plan for Hokkaido. By the 1970s, it was perfectly clear that economic growth in Japan was rather lopsided. Far too much activity was going on in the vicinity of Tokyo, Nagoya and Osaka (The Three Big Bays), while in other areas very little was happening. Hokkaido (Fig. 12.10), the largest and least densely populated of Japan's prefectures attracted the attention of the government as early as 1950, when the Hokkaido Development Act was passed.

Fig. 12.9 *Narita International Airport*

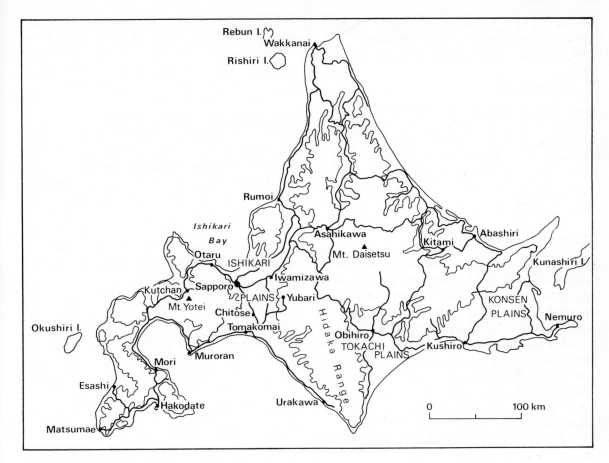

Fig. 12.10 *Hokkaido: general locations*

More recently, the New Development Plan of 1978 has set out a programme for growth in Hokkaido. The plan suggests four major possibilities for the years 1978–87.

1. *Primary activities*

Since Hokkaido has more usable space than any other prefecture, it is important that it should go on supplying food and raw materials to the more crowded areas of the country. Thus, the plan involves constructing new dairy farm villages in the Konsen area (see Fig. 12.10 again), and providing money for new forestry schemes. Around the coast there will be new fish farms and fish processing plants, with improved roads to link fishing ports to their markets. In addition, the plan supports continued mining for coal and ores in the Hokkaido countryside, and suggests offshore prospecting for oil.

2. *Manufacturing*

While the more crowded industrial areas of Japan might need to concentrate more on high-value products, there are other regions where the heavier, space-demanding industries need to locate. Hokkaido is one such region. The plan, therefore, suggests industrial expansion in two places: Ishikari Bay and East Tomakomai. In both cases, new harbours have been constructed to handle bulky raw materials, while new processing plants and roads are planned for the nearby coastal flatlands.

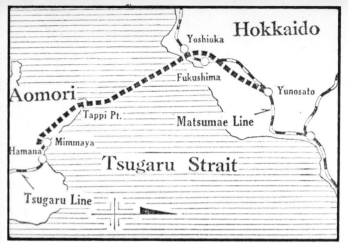

Fig. 12.11 *Location of the Seikan Tunnel*

3. Transport

If the inhabitants of Hokkaido are to enjoy the same standards of living as people elsewhere in Japan, the plan suggests that the island needs two types of transport improvement.

(a) *Internal*. Major towns need to be linked by modern expressways, like that planned between Muroran and Asahikawa. In farming areas, better quality roads are also needed, to link farmers with their customers.

(b) *External*. The island of Hokkaido is due to be joined by tunnel (see Fig. 12.11) to the Japanese mainland by the late 1980s. The Seikan Tunnel, the longest on earth, runs for 23.3 kilometres beneath the stormy waters of the Tsugaru Strait, and will connect Hokkaido with the main high-speed rail network of Japan. (Total length of the tunnel is 54 kilometres.) Another important development is the construction of the new Chitose Airport, near Sapporo, as the international air terminal for Hokkaido.

4. Amenities

The plan also outlines a number of ways in which life in Hokkaido can be made more attractive. Visitors to the island, for example, will be attracted in greater numbers if money is spent on developing new skiing areas (Fig. 12.12) and mountain resort villages. For people who live permanently in Hokkaido, the plan suggests improved medical facilities, more public open space in towns, and better community services (such as waste disposal and snow removal) for rural areas.

National planning

In spite of wide agreement in Japan about the need to reduce the imbalance between regions, it is important to realise how little has actually been achieved. Japan, of course, is little different from other countries in this respect. In Britain, for example, Scotland has received special assistance for many years, as has the Mezzogiorno in Italy. The results have been mainly disappointing, because these regions still suffer from economic difficulties and population loss.

Fig. 12.12 *Ski area*

During the 1950s, plans did exist to assist the less successful regions of Japan, but the main goal of the nation at that time was economic recovery and growth. Not until 1962 were the first real moves made to change matters. The National Development Plan of that year proposed new industrial growth in less congested areas, with restrictions on new expansion in the most crowded areas.

The 1962 plan relied heavily on the idea of *growth poles*, which British and French planners have also used. Two types of development area were to receive special attention, in order to help even out the differences in population growth and income levels between the richer and poorer regions of Japan. Hence, fifteen New Industrial Cities (NICs) and five Special Areas (SAs) were planned.

The NICs (Fig. 12.13) were made up of existing clusters of towns and villages in the more backward regions. Each one had access to the coast, where raw materials such as crude oil could be brought in for processing. The SAs (Fig. 12.14) were, by contrast, close to the large urban centres of the Tokaido megalopolis, from which industry and population could spill over into the new areas. For each development area, a target was set for industrial investment and population levels to be reached by 1975 and 1980.

As Fig. 12.15 shows, however, very few NICs or SAs have reached their targets, and in one case the population has actually dropped. The plan has fallen short for a number of reasons.

1. Most of the new investment was in heavy chemicals and metal smelting plants (Fig. 12.16) which, despite their great size, do not need large numbers of employees.

2. While the new areas did offer job opportunities, these were no better than the choices available in the Tokaido cities. Hence, there was little incentive for people to move from congested centres into the NICs.

3. Local people in the NICs and SAs were in many cases opposed to new indus-

Fig. 12.13 *New Industrial Cities (NICs)*

Fig. 12.14 *Special Areas (SAs)*

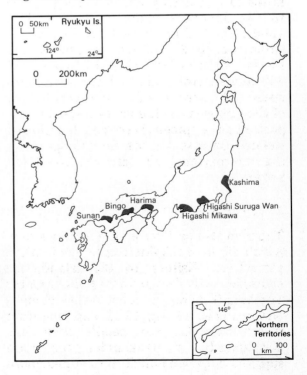

New Industrial cities	Actual population (000^s)		Planned population (000^s)
	1960	1975	1975
Do-ou	1292	2057	2069
Hachinohe	325	372	440
Sendai-wan	800	1015	1050
Akita-wan	298	347	430
Joban-Koriyama	823	831	1011
Niigata	697	779	900
Matsumoto-Suwa	526	579	670
Toyama-Takaoka	750	802	917
Nakanoumi	540	656	611
Okayama-Kennan	896	1176	1385
Tokushima	454	514	619
Toyo	486	497	638
Oita	446	551	640
Hyuga-Nobeoka	214	239	359
Shiranui-Ariake-Omuta	1514	1463	1662

Fig. 12.15 *Population data for New Industrial Cities (NICs)*

trial developments because of the air and water pollution problems which were being created.

In 1969, another phase of regional planning began, with the New Comprehensive National Development Plan. Among its chief aims was the improvement of the road and rail links between regions. It was followed in 1972 by an unofficial plan for *Building a New Japan*, put forward by former Prime Minister Tanaka. This, too, dealt with improving systems of transport and with relocating industry from overcrowded to underdeveloped areas. However, the fuel crisis of 1973–74 forced the Japanese to think again about how best to plan for the future.

In 1978, a new approach appeared in the Third Comprehensive National Development Plan. Its main feature is that it stresses the quality of life, rather than new industry, employment and greater

Fig. 12.16 *Oita industrial area, Kyushu*

wealth. This changed approach makes sense in the light of the many other changes affecting the Japanese economy. There are now, as we have seen, numerous laws to protect the environment from industrial pollution. Manufacturing in any case is now past its peak of growth, and light high-value goods are replacing the heavy products of former years. But, as the last section of this chapter shows, it is not only for economic changes that Japan has to plan.

Planning to cope with disaster

In Chapter 2, the section on weather and climate pointed out that Japan is open to natural disasters, such as severe storms and floods. However, weather is by no means the sole source of danger in the Japanese environment. The position of the country, at the junction of three great plates on the earth's crust, puts it at risk from several natural hazards.

1. Earthquakes

An earthquake is a sudden release of energy created by pressure building up in the crust of the earth. No country has as many earth tremors every day as has Japan. Most can only be detected by sensitive seismographs, and strong tremors, which might cause articles to fall from shelves, happen only occasionally, say, every few years. Disastrous earthquakes would occur perhaps once in ten years, on average.

During the twentieth century, the most devastating by far was the great Kanto earthquake of 1923, which was followed by fires that quickly swept through the lightly-built wooden houses. Two-thirds of Tokyo lay in ashes as a result, and 140,000 people died. Earthquakes on this scale cause floods from broken water pipes, fires from damaged gas and electricity lines, and the collapse of buildings. As ill luck would have it, the Pacific coast of Japan, with all its crowded cities, has a greater frequency of earth tremors (Fig. 12.17) than does the Japan Sea coast.

Earthquakes cannot be prevented, of course, but Japan has a national system of forecasting their occurrence. In addition, major cities have underground shopping centres, which are presumed to be less liable to damage during a major quake, and high-rise office blocks which incorporate special 'quake proof' building techniques.

2. Tsunami

When a large earthquake occurs on the deep ocean floor, it produces a form of tidal wave called *tsunami*. Out in the open sea, these waves are low and widely spaced, but when they reach V-shaped coastal bays the waves are compressed and their height increases. Hence, when the waves eventually break on the shore,

Fig. 12.17 *Earthquake locations*

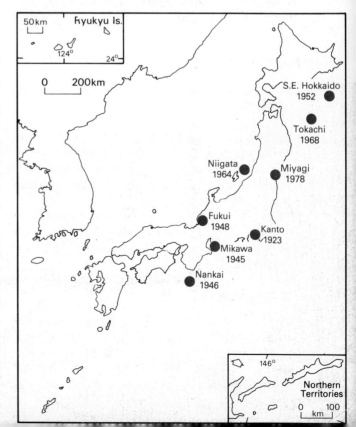

Fig. 12.18   *Showa Shinzan — a new volcano in Hokkaido (1943-45)*

they may be up to thirty metres high. This happened in the Sanriku disaster of June 1896, in north-eastern Japan, where thousands of houses and fishing vessels were destroyed, while over 20,000 people were drowned.

In more recent times, the Chilean earthquake of 1960 sent a powerful *tsunami* pulsing across the Pacific Ocean. Without warning, the wave struck the east coast of Japan, killing 139 people and wrecking homes, pearl beds and fish farms. It is difficult to plan against a hazard of this kind, but an international Pacific warning system has now been organised.

3. Volcanic action

Japan has about eighty active volcanoes (Fig. 12.18) which produce lava flows, mudflows, ash falls and clouds of steam. Many villages and arable fields lie on the lower slopes of volcanoes, as do several hot springs resorts. In previous centuries, volcanic eruptions on occasion killed thousands of rural dwellers, but the loss of life in recent years has been fairly low.

Violent volcanic eruptions usually give prior warning signs, and the Japan Meteorological Agency, therefore, keeps constant watch over the sixteen most hazardous volcanoes. Thus, when a large-scale eruption seems likely, local people can at least be evacuated from the vicinity in a planned fashion.

4. Landslides

These are common, for example, in hilly land where the underlying rock is soft or unstable. Any unusual event, such as heavy rainfall or earth tremors, can then trigger off a landslide. The city of Kobe (see Chapter 10) lies at the foot of the Rokko mountain range. When torrential summer rain falls, the short streams running down from the mountains have to carry too heavy a burden of mud and rock fragments. This material overflows from the stream beds, covering everything in its path.

In three disastrous mudflows and landslides (1938, 1961, and 1967), the city was extensively damaged, and over 700 lost their lives. In Kobe, as in many other cities, this is one natural hazard which has become more serious in recent times, as new housing encroaches further up steeply sloping land. The Japanese responses to the problem include laws which limit building in the most dangerous areas.

5. *Urban fires*

Fire is more of a man-made problem than a natural one in Japan, and accidental fires have been a traditional urban hazard. Modern cities are less vulnerable, but as recently as 1976 a fire destroyed nearly two thousand homes in the northern city of Sakata. To combat this danger, some local authorities organise a Disaster Prevention Day, during which the public are shown how emergency plans would work. These plans often include fireproof buildings for refuge, with underground stores of food, water and blankets. Fire dangers are closely linked to the earthquake hazard and thus, in the event of an earthquake warning, local television would urge viewers to shut off their gas and electricity supplies.

For similar reasons, concrete walls are a common sight at coastal locations, to reduce the problem of wave erosion and landslides. Again, on the steep sides of many roads and railway cuttings, protective walls and screens of wire netting help to lessen the risks.

Conclusion

In this final chapter, we have seen that Japan is a nation which looks seriously at planning for whatever the future may bring. The need to plan is obvious. As the Japanese population has grown to its present size, so the environment has been drastically changed. Urban expansion, the spread of industry and the reclamation of new land all seem to push nature into the background. Yet the natural environment will always make itself felt, whether in the changing seasons or in the sudden violence of earthquake and typhoon.

EXERCISES

Chapter 1

1. Consider some of the reasons which have made it easy for Japan to keep a regular check on its population numbers. You might refer to such factors as one language, few foreign immigrants, relatively small size of country.
2. Study Figs. 1.2 and 1.3, and then analyse the main factors which have caused the rate of natural increase to vary during the past hundred years.
3. In 1980, the proportion of children in the Japanese population was less than twenty-five per cent (see Fig. 1.8). Meanwhile, some Third World countries had over forty per cent of their total population in this category. List some reasons why the Japanese pattern might be preferable, in the light of such factors as health care, education and future employment or unemployment.
4. As life expectancy increases (Fig. 1.9), there will be very large numbers of elderly Japanese, some in poor health and many on low incomes. In what ways will this change affect the welfare services and the ordinary taxpayer? Consider some reasons why the graph of life expectancy cannot go on rising.
5. The overall population density in Japan (Fig. 1.11) is apparently lower than that of some other countries. Suggest some reasons why the Japanese national figure would not accurately reflect the real density.
6. Refer to Fig. 1.13. How many times higher than the national average is the population density in the Tokyo metropolis? What problems would you expect to result from such high densities?
7. Since World War II, large numbers of people have emigrated from Asian states, such as India, Bangladesh, Korea and the Philippines, in search of work. Suggest why Japan has not had a similar outflow of workers.

Chapter 2

1. In a generally mountainous country such as Japan, to what different uses might coastal terraces (see Fig. 2.7) be put?
2. Study Fig. 2.9, along with an atlas map showing the main cities of Japan. Which major city is located in each of the following lowland areas: Ishikari, Kitakami, Kaga, Kanto, Nobi, Tokai, Kinki?
3. Which type of air mass would bring the following weather conditions to Japan?
   a) extremely cold and cloudy, with snow flurries
   b) hot and moist
   c) cool and moist, with a mixture of showers and clear skies.
4. Study the following climatic data for Hiroshima and Sapporo, to identify the different air masses which most affect these two locations.
   Hiroshima (average monthly temperature and precipitation)

J	F	M	A	M	J	J
4.2	4.7	7.6	12.7	17.1	21.0	25.4
45	70	106	158	154	249	249

A	S	O	N	D		
26.6	22.7	16.7	11.5	6.6		
105	215	115	67	51	Total 1596 mm	

   Sapporo

J	F	M	A	M	J	J
−5.5	−4.7	−1.0	5.7	11.3	15.5	20.0
111	83	67	66	59	67	100

A	S	O	N	D		
21.7	16.8	10.4	3.6	−2.6		
107	145	113	112	104	Total 1136 mm	

5. Refer to Fig. 2.13, and then to a world map of ocean currents. Which two contrasting currents meet off the eastern coast of North America, just as the Kuroshio and Oyashio meet off Japan?
6. State the major hazard (as such floods, frosts or typhoons) which might be

reduced by each of the following measures: planting vegetables under vinyl sheets, strengthening river banks with concrete, warning the public by television and radio, building protective breakwaters at harbour entrances?

Chapter 3

1. Suggest some possible advantages and drawbacks of living on a small offshore island in Japan. What would be some of the problems involved in providing public services, including electricity, water, schools and hospitals, for such areas?
2. Compare the relative advantages and disadvantages of farming tuna fish and of deep-sea fishing for the same species.
3. From Fig. 3.4, identify those large urban markets which are also major fishing ports.
4. Study Fig. 3.5. Which type of fishing produces the highest value of catch per person employed? Which produces the largest catch, by volume? Which employs the largest number of people?
5. With the aid of your atlas, identify the following coastal ferry links: Osaka-Okinawa, Niigata-Sado Island, Aomori-Hakodate.
6. During a severe winter storm in 1953, the ferry *Toya Maru* sank between Aomori and Hakodate, with the loss of over a thousand lives. Identify the islands between which this ferry route operates. Identify the strait which separates the two islands, and name the tunnel which will help to reduce the chances of such a disaster ever happening again.

Chapter 4

1. Review the main reasons for Japan's traditional lack of pastoral farming.
2. Suggest some advantages and disadvantages of the ever increasing use of machinery and chemicals on Japanese farms.
3. In Japan, livestock such as pigs, poultry and cattle are usually reared on factory farms. In what ways might this system of farming benefit the public? What problems might it cause?

4. Examine Fig. 4.8. Which country might be able to sell surplus pulses (such as soybeans) to supply Japan's needs? Name two important cereals which Japan has to import? Again, which country might help to supply these cereals to Japan?
5. How true is it that *all* types of fruit production (see Fig. 4.10) increased in Japan during the period 1950 to 1982?
6. Is it inevitable that crowded countries cannot afford space for farm livestock (refer to the Netherlands in Fig. 4.8)?

Chapter 5

1. In which country was the largest number of Japanese metal mining projects located in 1979 (see Fig. 5.2)? Suggest two advantages (apart from ore deposits) which that country might possess for Japanese investors.
2. In which region of Japan did coal mining decline most rapidly between 1950 and 1978 (see Fig. 5.7)? List three or four local problems which would probably result from this decline.
3. What factors, beyond the control of the Japanese, might interrupt their imported supplies of coal and oil?
4. Outline three main reasons for Japan's decreasing dependence on imported oil?
5. Refer to the nuclear power stations shown in Fig. 5.12. What are the major advantages of the locations of these stations?
6. Discuss in detail the various advantages and disadvantages which the large-scale use of nuclear power can bring.
7. Review some of the ways in which conservation of energy is being achieved in Japan.

Chapter 6

1. In what ways is the overall organisation of Japanese industry different from that of British industry? Remember that in Britain most workers are in firms employing more than twenty people.
2. Many Japanese firms find it better to make workers completely responsible for the quality of what they produce. Why do you think this system might be better than the European and American system of

employing inspectors to check the quality of manufactured articles?

3. Suggest the probable advantages of Japan's policy of large-scale industrial investment during recent years (Fig. 6.3)?

4. Name three or four types of Japanese industry which have already been in decline, and suggest others which will probably decline in the near future.

5. Discuss the advantages (referring, for example, to transport costs, low pollution risks and low demands for factory space) of concentrating on high-value, low-volume manufacturing in Japan.

6. How does industrial inertia work to keep industries in certain locations, even when the original attractions of these locations have disappeared?

7. Study Fig. 6.10 Identify four different forms of manufacturing located in this area of reclaimed land at Kawasaki. Note that the word *kokan* indicates a steel plant. List some reasons why industry might find this a favourable location.

8. Study Fig. 6.11, and outline some of the factors which might attract industry to Nagoya. Mention port facilities, road links, labour and markets.

Chapter 7

1. Identify some types of service job which are likely to decrease in the future, because of automation.

2. With the help of Fig. 7.1, describe the main changes which have taken place in employment in Japan during the past century.

3. Consider some of the advantages and disadvantages of having many different services clustered together in the city bussiness distruct (CBD) of a large city such as Tokyo.

4. Many Japanese cities have large underground shopping complexes. What advantages does a modern shopping plaza offer? Bear in mind such factors as security, shelter and shoppers' convenience.

5. In which two areas of the world (see Fig. 7.9) does Mitsui seem to have its largest concentrations of offices? Which area seems least affected by Mitsui's overseas operations?

6. Write your own definitions of the terms *central place, hinterland* and *hierarchy of central places.*

7. Which of the following medical services would have the widest hinterland or sphere of influence: general hospital, local family doctor, specialised neuro-surgical unit?

Chapter 8

1. When we compare living standards in different countries, we often assume that material possessions are enough to make people happy. Why might this not be an accurate view of real life?

2. Make a balanced comparison between living standards in Japan and Britain, using the data in Figs. 8.7, 8.8 and 8.11.

3. In which main area of public spending would you say that Japan has been least successful during the past twenty years?

4. List some of the different ways in which Japan might benefit from its low rates of crime and vandalism (Fig. 8.17).

5. What are the main differences between the Japanese system of social welfare and the British system?

6. How true is the claim that Japan is a tightly-knit society, with few regional differences in language, no religious conflict and no great differences in social class?

7. Japan and Britain have borrowed various words and ideas from each other. Make a list of any Japanese words which you have come across.

Chapter 9

1. Study Fig. 9.2. Suggest some reasons why the problems of air pollution are generally more persistent during winter.

2. Suggest how waste heat from power stations could be profitably used in urban areas (for example in heating domestic water).

3. Discuss the ways in which compulsory pollution control, and its extra costs, might affect the profits of a manufacturing company.

4. List some of the questions which the local residents' association in a Japanese fishing village might want to ask a chemicals company about to build a large new factory nearby.

5. In what ways could each of the following groups make concessions to help reduce industrial pollution: company share-holders, trade unions, customers, tax-payers?

6. How could the amount of agricultural chemicals in the environment (Fig. 9.6) be reduced? What would the results then be on farmers' profits and on the prices paid by household consumers?

7. Sum up the main measures which have been taken to protect the natural environment in Japan during the past twenty years.

8. Referring to Fig 9.13, identify three examples of each of the following types of location for national parks: coastal, interior mountains, islands.

Chapter 10

1. What are the special features of the private car which have allowed it to dominate the transport pattern?

2. Study Fig. 10.2. How has the pattern of rail freight changed in comparison with that of rail passengers?

3. Study the topological diagram in Fig. 10.6. Count the edges and nodes as shown. Calculate a Beta Index, correct to one decimal place, for the area.

4. Consider Fig. 10.7. In what ways is it important to build bridges which will reduce the detours involved in certain road journeys? Take into account such factors as road safety, wear and tear on vehicles, fuel consumption.

5. In what ways can a new airport creat both benefits and hazards for people living in the immediate vicinity?

6. List the main advantages of container freight, compared with conventional ship-borne cargo. Think about speed of handling, security from theft or damage, numbers of employees needed and links with road transport.

7. Fig. 10.16 shows Japanese imports and exports, by *volume*. Is it fair to say that Japan imports only non-manufactured materials and exports only manufactured goods?

Chapter 11

1. Sum up the main functions which were carried out by Japanese towns during previous centuries.

2. Study Fig. 11.1. What are the different functions which the ancient capital city of Kyoto would probably have carried out?

3. Referring to the urban photographs in Chapter Eleven, list some of the main differences between Japanese townscapes and those of western countries. What are the major advantages which Japan gains from having so much of its industry located on the waterfront?

4. [sic]

5. How true is it to say that *suburban* migration has replaced *rural-urban* migration as the main type of population movement within Japan?

6. Sum up the main arguments for and against a policy of favouring the motorist by building, for instance, new dual carriageways, large car parks and by-passes.

Chapter 12

1. Using Fig. 12.5, identify the four prefectures with the most severe decline in numbers of farm households (1960-75). Do these prefectures share any common feature?

2. Amidst the general population decline affecting most of Hokkaido during the period 1960-75, some urban centres were clearly growing. Name any six of these.

3. Using Fig. 12.13 and your atlas, identify one main centre in each of the *new industrial city* zones. Note that in several cases the NIC is simply named after its main centre.

4. Consult Fig. 12.15. Identify two NICs which in 1975 were far short of their planned population targets. What common feature do these areas share?

5. During recent years, Rotterdam has been ahead of Kobe as the busiest port in the world. Suggest some factors which favour the location of Rotterdam. You might, for example, mention the different hinterlands of the two ports, their different connections with inland waterways and their contrasting physical sites.

6. Summarise the main ways in which the Japanese plan to counter the effects of natural diasters.

Acknowledgements

Andrews, R.L., 5.1, 5.6

Anglo-Japanese Economic Quarterly Review, 10.4

Bell, E. & Dunlop, J.S., 5.3

British Museum, 11.5

Brown, Les, 1.12, 1.17, 3.9, 4.1(a), 9.9, 11.10, 11.13, 12.7, 12.16

Dore, R.P. for farming case-study (*Shinohata*, Allen Lane, 1978)

Geographical Association (Geography, Vol. 67, 1982) for figs. 12.8, 12.10

Gumma Prefectural Office, 2.11, 4.15

Harris, C.D., 1.16

Hiroshima-Nagasaki Publishing Committee, 11.8

International Society for Educational Information, Tokyo, 2.4, 3.3, 3.12, 4.2, 4.7, 6.15, 7.4, 7.5. 7.15, 8.5, 8.22, 10.8, 10.14, 11.23, 12.9, 12.18

Ishimizu and Ishihara, 11.21, 11.22

Japan Information Centre, 1.13, 2.2, 2.7, 2.17, 2.19, 3.8, 3.11, 6.8, 6.12, 6.21, 7.7, 7.10, 7.12, 7.13, 8.21, 9.5, 9.11, 9.14, 10.1, 11.4, 11.6, 11.9, 11.11, 11.15, 12.11, 12.12

Japan Library Ltd., 1.14, 3.11, 3.13, 6.23, 8.20, 8.23, 9.10, 9.12, 9.16, 9.17, 9.18, 10.5, 11.20, 12.3

Japan Pictorial, 4.16, 8.2, 8.3, 8.4, 9.10, 9.16, 10.10, 11.3, 11.7, 11.14

Jiji Gahosha Inc., 1.4, 4.13

Jones, Cliff, 1.1

Johnston, B.L.C. & Reichl, P., 6.11

Kobe Port Authority, 10.15, 10.17

Kyoto Handicraft Center, 11.2

MacDonald, Don, 4.4, 4.17, 4.19, 12.4

Maraini, Fosco, 8.18

Mitsubishi Corp., 5.10

Mitsui & Co., 5.9, 6.20, 7.8, 7.9

Schwind, M., 2.8, 5.13, 11.1, 12.6

Smith, Howard, 4.1(b)

Smith, R., for farming case-study (*Koroso*, Dawson Press, 1978)

Index

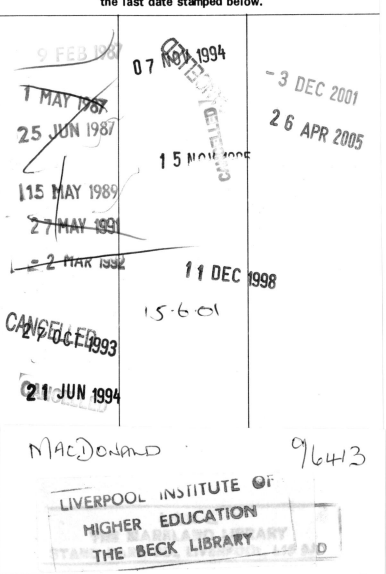